About the Author

Carolyn Hornblow is working as an Accredited Medium, Speaker and Healer of the Spiritualist National Union (SNU). For several years she has studied at The Arthur Findlay College, Stansted, England; an International Training Centre for Medium, Psychics and Spiritual Development. She has gained a Certificate of the Spiritualist National Union (CSNU)

In her earlier years, she trained as a Registered Nurse and Midwife in Edinburgh, Scotland. She also trained as an Intensive Care Nurse Specialist in Sydney, Australia.

She lived and worked near San Francisco, California for twenty years.

She ran her own Complementary Health Clinic for fifteen years in Scotland; specializing in The Bowen Technique. This therapy helps many physical conditions, primarily muscular skeletal problems. Gentle specific moves that encourage chronic muscular spasm to relax; allowing easier movement and reduction of pain.

Carolyn currently lives in Scotland, UK.

As a trance medium/channeler, she is able change her conscious level to an almost dreamlike state where she can hear voices from Spirit giving wisdom, guidance and various perspectives on how to live a better, more peaceful, and happier life.

These 'lessons or talks' can repeat in various ways. When she asked why, she was told that different people learn in their own unique way and one version would resonate with some and a different version with others.

GUIDANCE AND HELP FOR LIVING, FROM HIGHER REALMS, SPIRIT GUIDES AND ANGELS

Jim x
29/1/2024.

Carolyn Hornblow RN (ret_ CSNUi

GUIDANCE AND HELP FOR LIVING, FROM HIGHER REALMS, SPIRIT GUIDES AND ANGELS

Olympia Publishers
London

www.olympiapublishers.com
OLYMPIA PAPERBACK EDITION

Copyright © Carolyn Hornblow RN (ret) CSNU i 2023

The right of Carolyn Hornblow RN (ret) CSNUito be identified as author of this work has been asserted in accordance with sections 77 and 78 of the Copyright, Designs and Patents Act 1988.

All Rights Reserved

No reproduction, copy or transmission of this publication may be made without written permission.
No paragraph of this publication may be reproduced, copied or transmitted save with the written permission of the publisher, or in accordance with the provisions of the Copyright Act 1956 (as amended).

Any person who commits any unauthorised act in relation to this publication may be liable to criminal prosecution and civil claims for damage.

A CIP catalogue record for this title is available from the British Library.

ISBN: 978-1-80439-162-4

First Published in 2023

Olympia Publishers
Tallis House
2 Tallis Street
London
EC4Y 0AB

Printed in Great Britain

Dedication

I dedicate 'ANGELS SPEAK' to 'The Council of Twelve', a group of Ascended Spiritual Masters. Each have different specialities and wisdom. This group energy usually speaks as a group using the word "We." 'Saint Maria Magdalena de Pazzi', a 17th Century Carmelite Nun from Florence. Italy. Her feast day is celebrated each year in May. She is well known and revered in Italy and beyond.

'Abdullah', an Egyptian Alchemist. Tends to speak as first-person singular saying "I." Without their wisdom, this book would never have been written.

I also thank my many tutors who have helped me develop my gifts of clairaudience and clairvoyance; giving me confidence over the years.

Acknowledgements

With most grateful thanks to my friends Georgie Mabbs and Elaine Waller, who sat with me during these many talks. Their supportive energy and presence helped strengthen the connection with Spirit, increasing the power of these talks. Paul Challenger also produced illustrated examples from the talks. You will find these on Facebook under 'Spirits Guidance Extracts', which I really appreciate. My thanks also go to Ronnie McLean who advised me on grammatical issues and helped me in many ways.

My version of How to Meditate

During these talks there are frequent comments by Spirit to 'spend time with us'; 'ask us' They are encouraging you to have a little quiet time; to go inside yourself and contemplate, reflect, meditate, attune, sit in the Power. By doing this, you will develop an ability to hear your inner voice, attune with your Higher Self, receive ideas, reassurance, guidance from the Spirit Realms.

Keep it simple. Give yourself initially ten to fifteen minutes once a day, at a time of day when you know that you can be least disturbed by partner, child, pet, phone, work etc. Late at night you may be too tired. Unplug the phone. Ritual is not necessary, but can help. Lighting a candle in a safe container, incense if you wish. Music can be an aid but can be distracting to the subtle points and ideas and creative thoughts that will pass through your mind.

Get comfortable, uncross arms and legs and have your back straight. Sitting up is best I find. In bed with legs slightly bent or straight. Chair or cushion on the floor. If you can get into fancy poses, or very bent knees so be it, but being comfortable and warm is key.

Part your lips slightly. This helps the energies to move within you. Some say touch the tip of the tongue on the roof of the mouth. I find that letting the tongue hang in the middle of the mouth, not touching the roof of the mouth is easier and stops the mental thinking from going on. It allows for a quicker quieting of the mind to occur. I also use the tongue position if I cannot sleep for thinking too much and find it very helpful.

Then just BE, sitting not doing anything. You can take a few deep breathes and then breathe normally and just be in your own space.

Thoughts will come into your head; this is normal. Let them pass through your mind, like a cloud crossing the sky. Do not attach your mind to the thought, just let it pass.

If one thought is very persistent, quickly write it down on a notepad beside you for following up later. Once written down you will be able to let it pass. The focus is to slow down the thoughts more and more so the gap between the clouds (thoughts) is bigger and longer.

BE present for the present – you may see lights behind your eyes. You may see swirls of patterns; just go with it. You may get a sense of expansion, of inner warmth, lightness, a glow like sunlight coming behind your eyelids. You will, if you are like me, open your eyes to check if the sun has come out from behind a cloud. It may have; or it might be your own lightness of being making its presence felt. This helps you become aware that you are more than this physical body… so much more.

Set yourself a time for when you want to finish. You will find that you are drawn to ending at around that time. I recommend no more than half an hour for the first few months. If you find you wish to do more than that; then go for it.

Remember it has its own level of healthy addictiveness. So make sure you are not meditating at the expense of getting your regular everyday stuff done!

Enjoy learning that you have a fullness within, that still small voice of information, reassurance. You may not hear an actual voice but you may hear yourself thinking thoughts that inspire you. A knowing or a thought that you wonder where it came from; an inspiration, idea, creative image that you have never had before.

Take a few minutes at the end of the session to write down any meaningful experiences or ideas you came up with. You can also ask specific questions before going into meditation and may get the answers there and then or perhaps through a friend's comment, an article that catches you eye, a book you come across shortly afterwards.

Being in the 'zone' is a modern-day label for imagery and thinking yourself into a good functional state. It has been discovered that the brain has a 'plasticity'. So by visualizing and thinking of some action, for example running well; can make your body believe it is doing it. The power of positive thinking; 'being on the zone'

The difference between that and meditating is there is brain visualization and mental doing; versus reducing mental 'doing' and being brain still; which is not easy.

Both work well but the meditation and being in the 'ah' state is more for feeding your soul, your essence. Now if you did the meditation most days and then practiced being in the 'zone', you could well be unstoppable!

The chief reason for meditation I find is that it makes my day go better. I get less ruffled with the pressures of traffic, work, phone calls, other people's issues, I go more calmly through my day, worrying less about the extraneous issues. I achieve what I need to get done more effectively. I feel a warmth, an inner fullness, and am less tired. The stress factors are still around but they bother me less; I can shrug them off more easily. I am in more of a state of inner peace yet functioning at a high level. I have less need to fill up at the end of the day with excess alcohol, food and purchases. I snap less at others and as I am less snappy, others around me are also more comfortable, less fractious and more at peace and in harmony. Less yelling, shouting, blame, attacking goes on. There is less 'war' in my home and more peace.

'You can search out there in the world; then come home to find it within you.'

ANGELS SPEAK...

These are a collection of fifty channelled talks, trance speaking, to enhance your life. Some of the talks have a stronger influence from one or two energies. Essentially it is a teamwork of several energies blending together to pass on their wisdom to the human race. My voice was recorded during these sessions and then typed up later. The fifty talks cover a variety of topics spoken in a harmonious healing way. The topics touched on are how to live better and more fulfilled lives. Tools are given to help you discover your spiritual soul self; to nurture and take care of your inner self. How to find your life purpose and meaning and ways to enhance it.

Over many years I have developed the ability to go to a deeper level of consciousness where I can hear spirit guides and angels speak about life. This is called channelling, inspired speaking, trance mediumship. I am able, at specific times, to hear the voices of Spirit. This gift is called clairaudience. Having others present increases the power and connection for this communication. Myself and two friends met weekly.

The majority of these talks were produced during the Covid pandemic, where all restrictions were adhered to. We met via zoom and later in my garden and house. You can choose to read these talks from start to finish; maybe one a week. However, I would recommend that you open this book at random and see what speaks to you. I hope these talks will help you on your path through life; to achieve a more fulfilling, happier and enriched

life. Remember that you are a spiritual being, living in a physical body. You have been given the gift of life in which to learn.
AIM TO BE HAPPY.

Talk 1 – Sitting with Elaine and Georgie

15th June 2020

We give you greetings. We are the Council of Twelve and Abdullah. We're here to bid you a good day and to give thanks to you for coming to be here. We honour your presence. Realise that by being present in the moment, you give yourself a gift. The gift of presence, the gift of absorbing the now, being here now. There is nothing more important than that. From that place comes wisdom, awareness and realise you are giving yourselves a gift of yourselves. Your time in this present time, and again we thank you.

I am Abdullah. I used to be in what you call the Middle East. I used to be Egyptian, but as a spirit I have no nationality. I have expressed that I am interested in metaphysics, but I'm also interested in human beings. How they live their life, how to improve their betterment. How to give them tools to help their education and understanding of the universe, of their world and our world. I wish to speak of many things, but this would take time. I am pleased to be in your presence. I have also introduced our instrument to the phrase 'Ahlan wa Sahlan'[1], which in Arabic means 'Welcome' and indeed, you are most welcome. I also give thanks for your being present here, and now I wish to bring you

---

[1] An Arabic warm greeting meaning Welcome, Hallo. It also infers that 'you are with your people.' Usually said by Abdullah, the Egyptian Alchemist, at the beginning of each talk.

peace and harmony, and I hope that my teachings will help you to obtain that. I am sure you have a question regarding the infectious state that is on your planet at present. It is not pleasant but sometimes these things happen, when one must learn to deal as best one can with them.

There are blessings to be found during this time. Improved communications amongst people who are getting to know others better. Families learning to get along and communicate more, to play more, to treasure each other more. Siblings honouring siblings and parents; and parents learning to communicate on a different level with their children. This brings much enrichment to society. There is also the reaching out of neighbour to neighbour and friend to friend. This is good. The capacity of caring in human beings has been enriched and is being enriched. Too often, there has been too much busyness in life without the time to communicate with others and with oneself. This time of isolation from the normal has many enriching advantages. People caring and sharing as they would not normally do. People reaching to God more than they have been doing, because God was being forgotten in the business of life.

This time of quiet encourages you to search for more meaning in life. Why you are here, and why are you here at this time?

Each of you has a purpose, and your responsibility is to find that purpose, to find your way, your part. Are you doing what you are supposed to be doing? No judgement, no criticism is required. This should be done with love and care. Why are you here? How are you going to lead your lives from this point on?

What changes do you need to make or not need to make? Are things perfect just as they are? During this time there is a deepening of wisdom within. Some cracks that have been there before may become bigger cracks or may heal and become joined.

Nature has benefited in so many ways from this time. You have become aware of bird calls and songs more so than before. The sun seems brighter, the air fresher for it is so. Treat this time well. Nurture this time and allow creativity within you to blossom. Old crafts may be revised and revisited, and new crafts may be discovered.

Learning to enjoy the time on your own from time to time is good. Learn to cherish yourself, to nurture yourself. Only you can meet your needs at this time. Others may assist and help you, but now is the time to make oneself whole, to take care of oneself. This is not being selfish. This is allowing self-care so that you can then care more for others should they need it. An overfilled cup or heart pours more energy more easily than a drained one. So, nurture that cup of yourself, which is your soul, your spirit.

You are unique and you need to honour this fact. When we see you, we see you by your light, your spirit, your uniqueness. We do not see you as what height you are, what width you are, what colour you are. We see you as the light that shines from your heart, from your energy. Nourish the light within you. Imagine you are a crystal with many facets. Take time to polish the facets. No rush is needed. Simply allow the flow to occur. It does not have to be done all in a rush. Allow yourself time to nurture yourselves.

Talk 2 – With Elaine and Georgie

22nd June 2020

Greetings, my children. We are pleased to have you with us today. We are the Council of Twelve and we bid you welcome. I am Abdullah, and I also give my greetings to you this day.

Guidance is necessary during these times. It is good to turn towards Spirit to obtain guidance, to keep you steered in the right direction. Sometimes there is too much busyness, so to be calm, to be seated and to allow time to be, rather than doing, is good. This allows time for you to turn towards your spirit guides and to Spirit and God to allow for guidance, not control, for we cannot control you. You always have free choice for guidance, for help if you request. Listen to the inspirational voices that you hear, the still quiet voice, the impressions that are fleeting, your inner voice, your premonitions, your dreams. We can give guidance in many ways, through voices of other friends and loved ones, through something you read in a book. Keep your mind open, keep your vision un-blinkered, so that you can be aware of the signals we pass to you. For we truly walk the path together, spirit and human, because we are all spirit. It is just that some are in the body, and some are not. There is no separation. We always try to encourage and support but never control. This is your journey, and these are your decisions to make. That is why you have come to Earth, to explore, to play and learn. To learn the lessons, you cannot learn when you are in spirit.

Enjoy your time on earth, for this is a brief time in eternity. Yes, you will struggle, but not all the time and struggle encourage you to look at changes, to learn new lessons. If there were nothing to struggle about, you would never learn or not learn as much as is possible. I ask you, therefore, to spend some time each day turning towards your inner self, your guidance.

Do not make this rigid. There is no right or wrong way. It is simply to BE for a period of time. To allow yourself to hear, see or know what is right for you on your path. It may not be the right path for others, but for you, it is the right path. Trust your intuition, trust your knowing and not only trust but follow it, for it is a valuable guide for you.

Like a lighthouse that beams to you, the ship that is wandering on the ocean, they want to guide you and keep you safe. As lighthouses, the lights go on and off. You see them and then you don't see them. So, the guidance does not have to be constant; it can come and go. Just be aware that it is there, and it is your choice if you wish to look towards it and ask for its guidance.

None of us will force this on you but trust in your inner knowing; do not doubt it. Do not say, "it is just my imagination." Do not dismiss it like that. Trust yourself and be of good cheer. Be happy whenever possible. Where there are two paths open to you, take the path that will make you happy because life should be joyous, harmonious, and contented.

Yes, you may make mistakes. You are human. But is a mistake really a mistake? Or is it an opportunity to learn what does not work for you so that you can change direction and take a different path? So really, there are no mistakes. It is all opportunities for life learning discoveries. Some discoveries are uncomfortable, but that uncomfortableness makes you grow like the pearl and oyster. The pearl needs irritation to make it grow, and that is the way of nature.

Nurture yourselves. This is not being selfish. Nurturing yourself is necessary. There are many ways of nurturing. Being kind to oneself, taking care of yourself, loving yourself, being gentle with yourself. Not being too critical and harsh. Treat yourself as you would treat others, others that you like! You see, we have a sense of humour because some are harder to like than others.

As we said, be of good cheer for this is not the only path; the be all and end all; life continues on. This is just one of many schools or playgrounds that your soul can be on to learn lessons, to grow.

We are so pleased to have had this opportunity to come and share with you all, and we wonder if there are any questions you may have or if you want to wait for another time? It is safe if you wish to ask a question.

(Pause... xxxx asked a question silently and heard an answer.)

We thank you again for spending time with us, and we bless you

Namaste[2], Shalom[3].

---

[2] An Indian greeting used by Buddists and Hindus amongst others. It can be a simple greeting or more deeply saying 'The Divine within me bows to the same Divine within you'. Often said while holding both palms together in front of your chest in the position of prayer and bowing to the other person.

[3] A Hebrew word meaning peace, harmony, hallo or goodbye.

Talk 3 – With Elaine and Georgie

14th July 2020

DO NO HARM

Greetings, my children. We are the Council of Twelve, and we give you thanks for being present here today. And dear ones, welcome, 'Ahlan wa Sahlan', which is Arabic for welcome.

We want to talk today about the world. The world as you know it is a sphere that turns in the sky, in space, that is on an axis, an angle, which rotates. Not only does the world rotate but the axis also rotates over a period of time. Rivulets of water flow more and more into streams and rivers and into the oceans. The ocean is all one. You give it different names for different parts of the Earth, but it is all the same water wherein the fish can swim. Sea life is plentiful, with so many multitudes of fish in different forms. And deep-sea vents that allow the heat from the centre of the earth to come out into the water so that the earth does not overheat, allow spews/fumes of heat to release into the waters.

But there is too much pollution, too much silt, chemicals, and materials that do not belong in the waters. This pollutes the sea life, strangles, and kills. You must become aware of the chemicals as well as the plastics and strive to make the rivulets as clean as can be. Each of you must take responsibility, not just leave it for the other person. When you see rubbish on the beaches, pick it up, whether it belongs to you or someone else. If you can, carry it away. It is your responsibility, or your ability to respond, to pick up anything that might harm or pollute. Be responsible for your imprint on this earth. If you have the ability to do so, then do it. Do not presume others will do it for you. Do not presume that your waste will not make a difference. Every grain of sand gathering together can make a beach or a desert. Your grain of sand, your piece of dirt, can impact to make a difference. You are privileged to be on this planet. You have been given life so that you may experience what life is like. You can learn lessons that you cannot learn when you are in spirit. To have been given the gift of being present on this earth, you have a responsibility to take care of the Earth. You have more brain, more thought capacity than anything else on this planet, so it is your responsibility to take care of it. To take care of the animal kingdom, the plants. Do no harm, do no harm.

Do no harm to others, humans, plants, minerals, insects, ocean, birds. Take care of where you are. Command others to do the same. Help to make people aware, open their eyes so they then know and can become aware of this themselves. This continues the ripples of the waters, spreading out knowledge, information, consciousness, and awareness.

Be of good cheer for this is not a heavy responsibility. This can be done lightly with laughter, with joy, with challenge to see who can collect the most rubbish in their bin when you go to collect rubbish on the beach. Make a game of it; make it second nature.

Man has forgotten how to behave towards nature. To nurture nature, to do no harm. Because the harm that is done will come back to haunt you, it may not be today, and it may not be tomorrow, but you cannot continue to pollute the atmosphere without suffering the consequences of dirty air, which creates harm in your lungs. So, what goes around, you see, comes around.

You do not have to take care of the whole globe, just your part of the globe, your piece of land. Make it like heaven upon earth and share what you do with others so they become aware and so the movement grows. As more people become aware, so the earth becomes cleaner. Give thanks for the trees that are near you, the birds that you see. Appreciate them for they all have life in different ways. You have the capacity to think for all of them, to nurture and protect so that your footstep on this planet does no harm.

Step lightly on the earth and likewise nurture yourselves. Do no harm to yourselves. Take time to relax, to be, to nurture. Eat well and nourish your body and nourish your soul, your spirit, your brain. For you have been given the gift of a body, so take care of it. Treat it well for it is your home, a home for your spirit while you are here. Give thanks daily that you have been given this gift of life. For you have chosen to come to learn your lessons, lessons you cannot learn in spirit. Give thanks that you are here, and give time to nurture your spiritual self by connecting with the God that is within you, for you are truly a son and daughter of God.

So, bless that God particle within you that you are. Go forward, enjoy and be in harmony with yourself on the planet and your surrounds.

We give you more thanks again for being present.

Shalom [4] and Salaam [5].

---

[4] Shalom is Hebrew for Hallo, Goodbye but mainly Peace.
[5] Salaam is Arabic meaning Greeting, Peace

Talk 4 – With Georgie

13th July 2020

Greetings, my children. We are the Council of Twelve and we give you our greetings.

'Ahlan wa Sahlan.' It is I, Abdullah. I want to talk today about how the Earth revolves and has its place in the universe and how each planet has its right place in the universe. They are independent; each planet is independent of the others, and yet there is an intertwining, an interrelationship amongst all. There are beams of energy that spread out, like a vortex, across the skies, and they interchange and weave in and amongst the planets. The Hubble Space Telescope can peer into space, but yet it does not see everything. There is matter and antimatter. There are strands of energy that interconnect. There is like a structure, a substance that composes the space between the planets, an interweaving of matter, and each planet is perfect in its place.

There is a resistance, like a fabric, that creates support. If you like, it cradles each of the planets just like it cradles Earth. So, although Earth seems to be independent and revolving and moving, it is not as independent as it appears, for it is cradled with this matter. Archimedes touched on this and mentioned it and also the space-time continuum.

The vastness of space. There are other planets, other matter that is way beyond your knowledge at present and yet there is an intertwining relationship between them and your own planets, for all is connected, as humans are connected. Humans look different and there are so many differences, yet they are the same. So, it is with the universe. Different orbs, different planets, different sizes, yet each connected in various ways.

There are planets that you have experienced but do not remember. What today you call Earth is your planet, your home, and so it is. The universe is evolving as you evolve. Being here on this planet helps you develop and grow and learn and become wiser and expands your soul knowing. There is still so much to be learnt, but you are willing to be on your path, to learn, to dream, to have inspiration.

You must recognise the interconnectedness of all of you who are on planet Earth. Not just human to human but human to nature, to animals, insects, and microcosmic beings, all is one. It is important to nurture your true nature and to honour each other and your similarities; focus on that rather than your differences. For each of you is a spark of the divine and your spark is just as important as the next person's spark. Honour your spark, nurture it and be aware of it fully, for this is your true nature. Your body is simply a vehicle to help you be on the planet to function. When the time becomes right, you will discard your body and release yourself from it. But in the meantime, you must give thanks for it, for it is a temple; it is your soul's home. So, you must nurture it and take care of it.

There are no accidents. People die when they are meant to die, when they choose to die, when this current life learning is done, for Life continues for eternity. You will always learn, always develop, so honour your body while you are here and while you are here, honour your divine spark.

There will be divine sparks that have more affinity with you than others. It doesn't make others wrong or you right; it simply is. Souls can gather in groups, and if you are with your soul group and you will recognise those who are part of your soul group, then you will be comfortable and support each other. Everyone has a soul group that they belong to. There are multitudes of soul groups.

You are beings of light. Remember your lightness, your energy, your light spirit. We, in spirit, recognise you by your light, by your spark, and when you come back to us you will recognise us by our spark. You will know who you are, be more connected to your brethren and you will continue on together, learning, playing, and evolving. Support each other on your path, for you are all travelling together, some quicker than others. Some have been here (on Earth) more often than others, or will come with more wisdom, more knowing. Some are younger souls who have less wisdom at this time, and so it is. None of that is right or wrong; it just is.

Bless your being, bless your divine spark, your body. You are divine and all of you matters. In that there is balance. Over-focus on one part and you become out of alignment, out of balance. So, honour all parts of yourself and honour the paths that others are walking along. Each has their own path, their own development, and you may not understand why some choose one way and some choose another. But their spirit knows, their spirit understands, their higher wisdom understands. And you are all blended together, as is the universe, individuals yet one.

Balance is the key. Neither overworking nor underworking. Balance in nature. Harmony, like harmonious music, harmony is a vibration of balance. Notes come together to make chords, and where there is balance there is harmony, and where there is harmony there is peace.

As we said earlier, do no harm. Be harmonious. TRUST. Follow your instinct, your knowing. Trust that you are on the right path for yourself if you are following your inner guidance, your inner knowing.

Enjoy each moment of each day, for life is precious and time goes swiftly. Enjoy your time and take care of yourself and others.

Blessed be. Amen

Talk 5 – With Elaine and Georgie

20th July 2020

Greetings, my children. We are the Council of Twelve and we are here again today. We give you welcome and we give you thanks for being present. We are grateful that you are here, giving of your time, and we bless you for doing this. We sit in harmony with yourselves. When we come, we also bring your loved ones who also sit and harmonise with you during this work. So, you help us and we help you. We help you with your harmonising, with your vibrations.

Harmony is just like a chord of notes playing together, and when there is the correct harmony, there is a lovely vibration, not discordant; but an energy that helps open your heart, touches your spirit, your soul and brings peace and happiness to yourselves.

(Silence, and I am feeling a tremendous heat and hearing nothing… so there is a shift of energy.)

'Ahlan wa Sahlan.' It is I, Abdullah, here, present. The Council of Twelve, if you like, is my 'gateway' for me accessing and coming through, and I am indeed part of the Council of Twelve.

They were talking about harmony and vibration. Life has to do with harmony and vibration. Without vibration there would be no life. There are many levels of vibration, some fine, some coarse, some visible such as light, some invisible, such as infrared and ultraviolet. Invisible to you humans but visible to other organisms such as animals. There are spectrums, ranges of light from slow vibration to fast vibration. When the vibration becomes extra fast it can make heat, such as lasers. Vibration is an energy. It creates energy, heat, light, and life. Everything is energy. Without energy there would be no Earth, and we would all be dead.

I should say *you* would be dead because I am already dead, if you like. I am, in fact, very alive but you cannot see me. Because when you die, the vibration does not cease; it simply changes, it quickens. So, the slower vibration where you are visible as a body, you harmonise with the physical form so that you can live in it, be in it and move in it. So when it becomes time to move on or come over to the other side, you simply discard this bodily form because its matter is too dense. So you release it, leave it and transfer over. The vibration quickens; however, you are still the same, you are the same soul, the same spirit returning to us, to our side.

Even such things as rocks have vibration, crystals have vibration. The sky has vibration, and the Earth has also. When there is movement within the Earth, you can have the vibration that you call earthquakes, where there is a shuddering of part of the planet as adjustment takes place. There is always movement within the Earth, the heat from within the Earth, the movement of the seas, the wind on the land, the water running, you breathing.

The movement of the bloodstream, the pumping of the heart. And then, if you like, there is the heartbeat of the universe, for there is movement within the universe. There is energy, for as I have already said, it has to be everywhere, and it is everywhere. It just comes in different ways, waves, waveforms, frequencies and all are harmonised together so everything can coexist.

There needs to be more harmony within men… and women, but I will just talk about men in the generic form. There needs to be more harmony amongst men. More peace, more easy vibration, harmonising between nations, between neighbours. Fewer power struggles, less ego, more concern for others. More focus on peace, nurturing, harmonising, and working together for the good of the land and for the good of the planet. Cleaning of the oceans creates good harmony, and cleaning of the land does the same, removing the pollutants that scar the Earth.

Nature and nurture. Nurturing nature, nurturing yourselves, honouring nature, honouring yourselves. Ceasing in the abuse of drugs and alcohol for although this makes you numb, makes you not feel, and calms the mind, it is not a good way to live. It causes much disease and 'dis-ease'.

People have a 'void' in them, and they avoid this void in many ways. They need to search for their God in this void. They need to search for their spirit, their soul in this void. So rather than avoiding the void they need to sit and absorb the void, go into the void to learn about the sweetness within the void; the quiet, still voice of God, of spirit, the guidance that they can find within this void instead of numbing it out with too many things, too much food, too many drugs, whatever the numbing method happens to be.

They need to learn to enjoy each day, and *treasure* each day, for it is a gift, a gift that is given to you. Never assume that you will have the next day. You may well have the next day, however you may find that you are no longer in the physical form the next day, and then you will have missed out on opportunities that you can only achieve in the physical form, which is why you chose to come here, to experience, to learn.

So accept the rough with the smooth, but learn to *feel* the void, not to avoid it. People should have classes about the void so that maybe they would turn inward to learn, to be comforted, to see their light, their wisdom within, rather than avoiding that by other means.

The art of living is to discover this before you come back. That is part of life's journey, to discover that you have heaven within you. You do not have to wait to get to heaven. To learn to harmonise as a spiritual being on the planet as a physical being. For the two parts of you to be in harmony, your physical and spiritual sides to walk as one. Being conscious of both aspects of yourselves on a daily basis and honouring both aspects. There needs to be balance. You should neither be too physical nor too spiritual; balance is the key. That is where harmony comes around, where there is balance.

Love yourselves, nurture yourselves so that you can love your neighbours and love your friends, and with that love radiating out from you it will spread like ripples into the communities. You can not affect the whole Earth, but you can affect the part that is near you by your presence, by your caring, and this will spread out to others who will resonate with your resonance, and they, in turn, will resonate harmony with their friends and relations and so the harmony will spread and radiate out further and further.

And so life will become more illumined, more light, more wisdom, more harmony, more singing of the soul amongst you all.

You are in a privileged place being a body, a spirit in a body on the planet Earth. It is your responsibility to take care of your body, to nurture your spirit. To grow in wisdom and harmonise with your neighbours and friends. Help to create the harmony of the planet.

You *do* make a difference, each one of you. Like a web, if one strand is pulled in a web, it pulls the whole web. So you see, each one of you can make a difference.

And if you find yourself in disharmony, go within to find out why, because your natural being is harmonious. So often dis-ease and disease are caused because there has been a lack of harmony, a problem with the vibration of the body, which affects the flow of energy, and can be the cause of illness.

Balance your time. There is a time for playing, there is a time for work. There is a time of being, there is also a time of doing. Balance and harmony reduce illness, disease and dis-ease.

Harmonise your lives, your planet, so that ripples of energy and peace can be felt.

Honour your void and learn from it. Do not numb it out. Salaam.

Talk 6 – With Elaine and Georgie

28th July 2020

Greetings, our children. We are the Council of Twelve and we are glad and pleased to be with you today, and again we give thanks for your company. I am Abdullah. 'Ahlan wa Sahlan,' and I too give you my greetings as I have already done in Arabic, but it is good for me to speak and give you greetings in your mother tongue.

I want to talk today about the universe, the universality, the whole universe, the worlds upon worlds, universes upon universes, for there are more than one, there are many, and they all coexist together and combine together to work in harmony. Each has its own energy, its own orbit, and yet it is stable, allowing for other planets and other worlds to also be present, yet not clash. Infinitesimal points, stars, lights, globes, each with its own energy, its own resonance, similar yet different; there is balance. To use the phrase 'what goes around comes around'; if you exert evil on the Earth there will be retribution, Cause-and-Effect. Some nations call it karma; we call it balance. If you throw a rock into water the water ripples then becomes calm again. That is an effect. The rippling is the effect; the cause was the rock being thrown into the water, which caused the disturbance, caused a ripple to occur, and then the ripples get less and less until the water surface becomes calm again. Tadpoles wriggle and their tails fluctuate evenly as they travel, and then they progress and become frogs, tails become legs. If you observe the tail of the tadpole, the wriggle is balanced and so the head of the tadpole goes straight. If the tail was not wriggling in a balanced way, the head of the tadpole would go off to one side or the other and it would be out of balance. That is why it's important to have balance within your lives, so that things run smoothly and do not go off to one side or the other. There is progress as the tadpole becomes the frog, and so there is progress in the universe as things advance. Spectrums develop, light is split into many forms of colour and energies and each colour has its own vibration. And so too, each planet has its own vibration separate from its neighbour, unique. Each has a purpose, there is a reason for each to exist. Nothing is done by accident; there is purpose. There is always a plan in the cosmos, a natural event.

Without God there would be no harmony. God being a universal energy, universal consciousness but primarily a universal energy which creates the harmony, the balance, and the order of things. And as harmony is required on Earth, so it is in the heavens. A harmonising of vibrations so there are no clashes. All work together in unity. So, you see, each of you can have a different voice, have a different vibration, and yet you can be together in harmony. For you all have a body, yet each body is unique, each body has its own gift, its own learning, its own soul, and you harmonise with souls that have a similar frequency and vibration, so again there is no clash. You can coexist with others that have a clash with you for a period of time, but then it becomes too uncomfortable, so you choose to be more in harmony with souls that harmonise with you, that resonate with you.

And then you have Soul Groups, those of you that gather together when you are in the universe, when you are not in body.

Those of you that choose to come to Earth together over a period of time to support each other in your learning. There is a recognition when you meet up, a resonance, a coexistence where you help each other to learn, to navigate the way through the journey of life. Some of you will be siblings, family, and some of you will be friends. Some of you will be together for a long time, and others may just be brief, but it is all perfect, it is all as it should be. For there is a wisdom in the universe, a functioning that makes sense. Sometimes you cannot see that functioning, the sense, and you wonder why? Sometimes you become aware of why as you journey. Sometimes it is unknown until you come back to us, where you can see the full picture, the full tapestry of your life. Where you can see there are no accidents and there were no accidents; everything was meant to be.

It is important to nurture peace, for without peace there is no harmony. We have discussed before how creating peace within your environment then has a ripple effect, like the stone in the lake, in the pond. You are the cause by being in a good vibration, by being at peace within, extending the peace without to your friends, family, and community. And that peace then ripples and has an effect on others, and they then spread out... so you see it is cause-and-effect again. You have an effect on others, you are the cause, and this is a responsibility.

The word responsibility can seem heavy but in fact, it is being able to respond. It is an ability to respond, responseable. So, once you become aware of your newfound wisdom and awareness, you can then make a difference by acting and being different, and that is how you become a good cause and create a good effect. Harmonising with each other, being in balance yourselves and then being in balance with others.

We have talked about nurturing yourselves and nature and nurturing your void. Light sparks that you are, you help to lighten others. You enlighten them and help them become aware. One candle lit in a darkened room can bring light to another. As the light spreads the room becomes illuminated and bright. So, from darkness there can be brightness, and so it was when the universe began. There was darkness, and then there became brightness.

There is structure in the universe, building blocks if you like. There is substance that is like a web, so where you see space there is, in fact, solid; it is filled with matter. Some planets give life-giving energy, and other planets do not. There *is* life on other planets, but not as you see life here on this planet; because each planet, as I have said, has a different vibration. So, what can exist on the Earth planet cannot necessarily exist on another planet, but other forms of energy can exist. Other wisdom can exist on other planets, and there can be an exchange of information from one to another, as indeed there is on some planets already.

When you become spirit with us, you have learning potential, and opportunities, both here in our universe and also in other universes, on other worlds. The planets that you choose to go to give you different lessons. If you like, the planet Earth is somewhat of a playground. Remember to play and enjoy your life. Life should not be serious. Life should be a balance, as we have said before, of work and play, of busyness and stillness.

Be of good cheer. Lift your vibrations with laughter and joy. Try to help those that are having a struggle but do not allow them to drag you down as well, for that is not the purpose of life. Extend a warm hand but do not do so to the point where you suffer.

There is a time to let go sometimes and to realise your limitations. Realise that others maybe can help where you can't.

This does not make you wrong. It just allows you to have the wisdom of knowing your limitations. Neither should you ever allow yourselves to be abused, for that damages the soul and the spirit.

Treasure yourselves, for you are precious. We love you. We watch over you, we walk with you. Never forget to ask us for help should you need it. Never feel that you have to walk alone. You always have choice and trust that you are in the right place, right now. And if you are not at ease, if you are at dis-ease, then seek to see how you can change that. Treasure yourself enough to make a change, should you need.

We treasure you and we love you, and we wish for you to treasure and love yourselves also. Loving yourself is important; it is not selfish, it is important. Do not seek so much to get love from others because it will never be enough. Your love should come from within; love of self. You see, you can love yourself and not be selfish. Again, it is a question of balance. There is a difference between selfishness and self-love, and when you are in self-love you are more balanced and more in harmony. By being that, you can do more good to yourself and others that are around you.

Love is universal harmony. Love is the most beautiful resonance of all, so love yourselves and be at peace.

Amen, Shalom, Salaam.

Talk 7 – With Elaine and Georgie

3rd August 2020

Our Father who art in Heaven, hallowed be thy name. Thy kingdom come and Thy will be done on Earth as it is in Heaven.

Greetings, our children. We are the Council of Twelve and we come forward and bless you and thank you for your presence. I am Abdullah. 'Ahlan wa Sahlan,' and I also bring you my greetings.

There is a wisdom, an energy, a force that dwells in the universe. The wisdom that makes the trees go up creates Nature, and puts things into balance. This energy is given many names, God, Allah. It is a wisdom, a knowing, centre of the universe, the Creator, Divine One, Source, and we revere this energy. We respect it. It is our guide, guiding light. There is a range of energies that exist in the universe, from good to not-so-good and our aim is to aim towards the good, as should your aim be also. So, look towards the light of God of the heaven, of the universe and aim your arrow if you like, aim your focus towards that goodness. Aim to be as good as you can be. This does not mean you have to be perfect, for you learn by your imperfections, but we ask that every day your aim is to be as good as you can be. Direct your consciousness towards the Light, towards your spirit self. Acknowledge who you are, who you truly are. Acknowledge that you are only transiently in this body, that your soul lives forever. There is no death, there is merely the passing through the veil from body to no body, but your essence, your soul, your being is continuous; you live forever. Your aim should be that you develop as best you can. Correct errors of your ways. Apologise to your brethren, your brothers and sisters, if you should hurt them. Forgive those that hurt you, realise that they are working within their own limitations, and allow yourselves to move on, to move forward and enjoy the journey. For the journey of life is truly a miracle. The fact you even managed to arrive here on this planet in physical form is a miracle of its own. All the lessons you learn as a child, as you fall and get up again, as you absorb information and knowledge like a sponge. As you learn and grow. Then you, in turn, become parents and guide and help the little ones with their own learning and growing and experiencing. But even though you become an adult and can teach your children, you also are always learning. For life is evolutionary, you never stop learning unless you choose to close the shutters. You always have the choice to learn. Only you can choose to stop that and what a shame that would be, to stop your learning. For every day is a new learning experience, an opportunity to learn. Learn by your mistakes, learn by your omissions, learn by your play, your laughter, for life should be joyous in the main. Like a boat sailing on the ocean, sometimes the waters are smooth, the sun is shining and the wind gentle. Other times the sea is rough, there is rain rather than sunshine, and you are tossed about. But then the sun returns, the winds calm down, and you again continue on your sail through life.

Learn to make your sail full. Fill it up with experience. Do skimp on your experiences. Make the sail as broad as it can be so that you can move forward easily and use everything for your assistance on your journey. Use everything as an opportunity, a force, a forward movement, for nothing is wasted.

Even if you have to change course because you find yourself on the wrong course, that is all right too. Even if you change course two or three times, you will find that you are always tending to go forward, just maybe on a different track, different course.

So, when you sail into home, you can say to yourself, "That was a full life. I experienced so much. I learnt so much."

Try to find out why you are here, why you chose to come here, so that when you do sail into home, you can say, "And I learnt what I came for."

And when you sail into home, there will be so much rejoicing of friends and family that has passed before you. They will rejoice with you that you have come back to them.

And then you will settle for a while and absorb the lessons you have learnt in this lifetime. And when you are ready you will move on further, for life is always about learning, whether you are here on this planet or whether you are with us, in spirit, in the universe.

Be open to your intuition, be open to your knowing, for this can guide and help you. Try to spend a little time each day with us, by meditating, by contemplating, by observing, by being at peace, and pausing for a little while. For we can then help give you messages, information, inspiration, aha moments that can help guide you.

You will return to us when your time is right. It may be short for some and longer for others. But there are no accidents; things happen as they are meant to happen. Mistakes are learnings, maybe not the learnings you wanted, but they are learnings, lessons, and information.

Allow yourself the space in which to learn. You do not have to be perfect. You do not have to get everything right. Life is an experience. Try to enjoy your time on Earth. Remember, this is a school of learning, a classroom, a kindergarten even.

Be of good cheer and *lighten up*. See the light that you are and lighten up. By this we mean to enjoy your life, your journey. Try not to over worry, over fret and try not to overextend yourselves. We have talked before about balance. Play and learn. Know that you are Light, know that you are a particle of the universal knowing, the universal consciousness. And seek for that light, not only in yourselves but in others that walk with you, for you truly all are one. All experiencing life in its many forms, no matter what colour your skin, no matter what sex, age, or religion.

You are universal beings, respect each other, respect your differences. For everyone has something to teach, everyone has something to learn, no one has all the answers. Seek within for your own answers, for your own guide is your soul and spirit. So look within for your inspirations, your guidance; respect your void.

As the waters come in and go out, you will notice that your life has ebbs and flows. Ebbs at times and is quiet; other times it comes in and is full, in full flood. This is just the way life is, peaks and troughs, ins and outs, night and day.

Respect yourselves and respect others. Each of you can learn from the other. Be considerate of others and be considerate of nature. Do not harm your surroundings, take care of where you live, for it is God's gift to you to be here. You are fortunate to be in the physical body, having physical experiences. Do not waste the time, embrace it, and remember your Father, who art in heaven. Because that is your aim, to try and perfect your soul, and it doesn't happen in one lifetime; it takes eons of time. And remember, you are not sinners, no one in the spirit world labels you sinners. You simply make mistakes, which is human.

But do no harm to others, for this is not only injury to them, but it is injury to your soul, to your spirit, to your essence. Be at peace with others and with yourself. Harmonise with all, Man, Animal, Plant; Mineral, Earth and Sky.

And when winds of change come along, allow yourself to be flexible. Change always occurs. And when it starts to occur, look within, look within your void, your learning and see where the change is leading to, why the change has happened, and what learning you can come around to. Allow yourself to flow with the change, bend with the wind, and then your battle will be less. Like the Willow tree that bends to the will of the wind; after the storm it is still there. Unlike the Eucalyptus, which finds itself unable to bend and so often breaks.

Never let your spirit and soul be broken. Bend with the wind and look towards the Light. Learn and enjoy yourselves while you are here on planet Earth.

Amen, Shalom and Salaam.

Talk 8 – With Georgie and Elaine

10 August 2020

Dear children, we give you our greetings. We are, as you know, the Council of Twelve, and we are here to harmonise with you today. To be in your presence and give you our presents, our gifts to you as thanks for what you are doing. Blessed be.

I am Abdullah, and I too give you my greetings, my welcomings, 'Ahlan wa Sahlan'. I come today to talk with you about physics. The physical mass that you are as a body so that you can be on this planet, functioning. And also, the physics of Heaven and Earth, the rightness of things, the balance. For if the cause was incorrect, the effect would also be incorrect. We talk about Heaven and Earth, and yet there is very little separation between the two. All is material, all is substance. Some of it heavier than others. The blue of the sky and the green of the grass. It is all substance or material matter, matter that vibrates at a different frequency. The Earth frequency is heavier and slower than that of the sky frequency, and we have talked about harmonics and the harmony of things working together. The Sun rises on your side of the Earth in the morning, but as it rises here, it darkens on the other side of the Earth. Again, balance of night and day, day and night. The rotation of the planet in balance, allowing equal time of day and night throughout the Earth and the seasons of spring, summer, fall and winter. Extremes of weather in different parts of the Earth and less extreme in the middle. There is overheating of your Earth at present, and we are aware of efforts being made to try and counter this. Yet there have always been cycles of extremes of weather, whether it be heat, coldness, or wetness. Areas that are now desert used to be underwater, so you see there is always change; change occurs. And then other change occurs to redress when things become out of balance. However, it is good to make corrective changes whenever possible. To reduce the negative effects of excessive heat. To reduce the effects of excessive sun rays. To heal the sun barrier so that you do not get overheated, or over burnt.

This pandemic, as you call it, in fact, has caused healing on a different level, as there is less pollution of the skies and the seas occurring at this time, which is good for the planet and its healing. There have been other pandemics throughout the centuries, but corrections have been made and the world moves on. Given time, this pandemic will become history rather than current time.

Black holes are areas where energy changes and yet function still occurs. You could look at this pandemic as a black hole, a darkness where people are in fear and are dying and suffering. But there will be a rebalance, a healing, in time. Those souls that pass over are well received on our side, although we know that there is much suffering and loss to those who remain behind. Realise that those who are suffering now will be reunited with their loved ones who have already come over to our side. So grieving is appropriate but over grieving is not necessary because there will be a reunion. Over grieving impacts too much upon the life you are having as a person on the planet. Allow that change occurs and do not get stuck in the pattern of grieving. Allow yourselves to grieve, to remember, to think of and enjoy the fact that you knew and had time with the people you have lost and that you will reconnect. Allow yourself to move forward; do not get stuck in that pattern of grieving constantly.

Allow yourself to remember and allow yourself to move forward, for there are other opportunities and lessons that you can learn while you are still on the planet. The ones, your ones, who have already gone over would not want you to stop living *fully* just because they are no longer in your realm of sight. Because they truly do travel with you and visit you.

So, allow yourself to keep moving forward, learning, playing, enjoying, and being 'in joy'. Because that is what the word enjoy means, it is being 'in joy'. That, wherever possible, is your life's responsibility, to live every moment, embrace every moment, and enjoy every moment.

The Sun shines upon you and then the Moon shines upon you. There needs to be this balance because constant sun would be too much, for you need rest, and it is hard to rest when there is full sun upon you.

So, again, it is balance, time to work, time to play, time to sleep, to dream. Make sure that you get enough of sleeping. Again, not overmuch, but enough so that you can function optimally. Too many of you are too busy, and you will allow yourselves not to get enough sleep and rest. This is not good for you. It ages you too quickly. It causes stress which is harmful to the body. Your sleeping is important, it replenishes the cells in your body, and it allows you time to dream and assimilate information.

Each blade of grass has a purpose, as do you. You look upon a lawn and all you see is green; but in that lawn are many, many blades of grass. Likewise, you look upon a crowd of people and you cannot count them, and yet each person in that crowd is important, has a life, has a purpose, and has a reason for being.

Find out your reason for being, your purpose, so that you can then explore it, develop it, and nurture it. So that when you return to us, you are full of knowledge, achievement, and growth. Otherwise, it would be a wasted opportunity, a wasted journey, for although you will have learnt things, you may not have achieved the main reason why you chose to come to planet Earth. So, give time to your 'void', give time to your inner voice, because by doing that, we can help you remember the reason you came, through inspiration, intuition, knowing. Recalling your dreams can also help because dreams can give you information.

Use everything to your advantage, not in a selfish way, but in an all-knowing, all-seeking, all-finding way. As the Earth spins and the planets turn, you also move, spin, turn and learn. You constantly grow through your mistakes, your experiences, and your learnings. Even what appears to be a mistake to you is, in fact, a learning for your soul and spirit.

There are no accidents. And you are not an accident; never believe that of yourselves.

You are a precious being and you have a right to be on this planet. You have a right to stand in your power, own your power, claim your power. Do not hide your light. Let your light shine forth because you truly are light. So 'enlighten' yourselves with wisdom and experiences and claim your right to be here. Do not be a shrinking violet. Stand proud. For you are spirit in a physical body, and you are here to learn and to remember that you are indeed light in a physical body.

Enjoy your experiences and know that you will come home when your time is right, and you have learnt enough. Embrace those you love and share your love with them, for there is never enough love expressed in this world. Always let those that you love know that you love them. So that you can never regret, once they are gone, that you didn't let them know that you loved and cared for them. For love is the true healer, and love comes in many forms and many ways. So, love yourselves as we love you and surround yourselves with love, other friends and family, and love of life.

Breathe deeply of life and remember you *are* Light; you are a Light Being, a Child of God.

Amen, Shalom, Salaam.

Talk 9 – With Georgie and Elaine

17 August 2020

'Ahlan wa Sahlan.' This is I, Abdullah. I am here. Welcome, little ones. We are the Council of Twelve and we welcome you this day and we give thanks to you.

Wisdom, the wisdom of the universe, the wisdom of the world and the many worlds that are out there. And the wisdom of yourselves and humans. There is innate wisdom within you. Wisdom that you forget when you come here and your chore is to remember the wisdom, your intuitive selves, your knowing selves. For it is that wisdom that will drive you forward, drive you on your path. Allow that wisdom to be there with you daily. Do not tune it out, do not ignore it. Allow it to be there, be conscious of it. Make yourselves conscious of it by pausing, stopping for a period of time and become all-knowing. Allow doubt to stay at the door, allow trust to enter. Have faith, faith in yourselves, faith in your wisdom, faith in your knowing. Occasionally you might be wrong, but usually you will be right, and the more you sit and develop it the more you will discover that you are right.

Seek communication with the All-Knowing, the Mighty Presence, the Creator, the Essence of Being, which is given many names. It is the one true light of which you are a particle. You are told that God made you in his image. It is the light within you that is the image, not your figures. Imagine that light within you;

know that the light is within you. Be the light, for you are the light. You are a reflection of the God force whose light shines forth. Who allows the universes to spin, harmonise, balance, be the wisdom of the universe? I should say universes, for there are many.

We've talked about harmony before, but harmony is the key. Like black and white they are poles opposite, and yet they balance together to make a whole. Positives and negatives harmonising together to be complete, to be as one.

Aeons of time. We in spirit have no time, for time is a human invention; that is necessary for function on your planet. There is now and now and now, present time always. Too much time is spent looking back or looking forward but not looking at the present time, and yet all you have is present time. There is nothing else. So be conscious in this present time, cease to keep your consciousness in the past or the future because then you will miss the present. Be present every moment, be aware of who you are, what you are and why you are here, so that every movement becomes sacred, thoughtful, and meaningful. Your interchanges with each other take on a significance, so that you cease to waste time because time is precious. You have an interlude of time on this planet, an opportunity to grow. Do not waste that gift that has been given to you, and yet do not drive yourself too hard. Allow yourself playtime, resting time as well as learning time; such is balance. Enjoy your time. We have said this before, but it is most important to remember. This is time to have fun and learn and be. Because you have been given a period of time to be on this planet so, do not waste it. So that when you re-join us you will rejoice in your full learning, your full experience. You will have other experiences but right now, at this time, you are here on planet Earth. So, take full advantage of this time. Be a human being because that is what you are. A body and spirit exploring this Earth and be kind to this Earth.

Take care of it, take care of your universe, your world. Never have to be ashamed of your action, your lack of caring. Because sometimes you will make mistakes, for you are human and you are not perfect. And we do not desire you to be perfect because you are here in a school of learning where perfection is not necessary.

We all try to be perfect, even those of us that are in spirit, for we all aim to become closer to the Godhead. To become more at one and with one with the Godhead; clearer, more knowing, more perfect. We all have to strive at this at many different levels, and you will continue to strive once you have passed through planet Earth, for there is always learning and living an existence. You are energy, and as energy you will continue on, in different forms, as different beings.

Each planet has its own function, its own energy. And yet there is harmony with the planets, they co-operate. There is the word 'manifold', and we want to talk about the many folds of energy within the universe, the waveforms. Particles of energy that intertwine with each other, causing harmony and being harmonious. Movement exchanging, dancing with each other. As you dance on Earth the Universe also dances with energy.

Because energy is all that is. Different forms of energy, different frequencies.

So, there is matter that you see that is solid, or appears solid, and yet it is at a vibration that appears solid, and then you have energy that you cannot see as a solid form, for its frequency is different. Most of you cannot see us, Spirit, because mostly Spirit resonates at a different frequency than what you do as human beings. If you resonated as a Spirit, on human level, on this planet

Earth but without a body, you would not be able to achieve very much. So, your body is important, and it is important to treat your body with respect. Because, if you like, it is a vehicle with which you can be here on Earth. So, it is important to take care of your vehicle and love it. For it is allowing you to be here, no matter what colour, how tall, how thin; it is your body, and it works for you. So, respect it and take care of it. If you like, it is your gift that you have been given for a short time, which you will discard when your time of learning on this planet is over, and you, the real you, will continue on. You will come back to us for more learning, for reconnection with your loved ones.

There is a glow of energy around you, and there is a glow of energy around the planets. A liveness, form, a pattern of energy and nothing is separate; all is connected. When you talk of things like space, some of you think of a void, an emptiness and then a planet here and a planet there. But in truth there is a manifold, a material form of energy that holds things together. Allows for the positive and the negative and allows for balance and perfection. For birth, for dying of stars as they explode, implode, and are reborn into different forms of energy.

You have had many prophets that had been in human form on your land, and it is important to learn from all of them, for they all have messages. Do not negate some, for each has a message, a learning. So, learn what you can from different sources and again realise your interdependence with other humans, other learnings. You are all one, learning in different ways. None is wrong, no one has all the answers. The only wrongness that there is, is to do harm to yourselves, to others and to your planet. Be the best that you can be every moment but do not demand perfection from yourself because you are a child of God.

So be gentle with yourself, love yourself and be at peace with yourself.

Use your wisdom, your wise-ness, your inner knowing. It is your guide and helper on this path you are currently on.

Amen, Shalom, Salaam.

Talk 10 – With Elaine

24th August 2020

Greetings Children. We are the Council of Twelve and we harmonise here together with you today, and we give you our thanks for being present.

(I really feel a heaviness in my legs that I haven't felt before.)

Harmony and Wisdom and Being at Peace.

It is important to be in a state of peace as often as you can be. This is not always easy, for disturbances come and go. Seize the moment, be in the moment and be aware of trying to stay at peace within. Being in harmony with yourself and others. Being like the eye of the storm where there is stillness and peace in the middle of the cyclone and the tornado. By your peacefulness, centredness and groundedness, you create an energy that allows others to be peaceful around you. So, they learn from you. So often it is not the words you say but the way you *are* that teaches others. Be like the still pond with a few ripples on the surface. Give yourself time to remember your stillness, your wisdom, your inner knowing. Never presume it will always be there. You have to nurture it and develop it so that when the wind comes and blows, the ripples are not too many. The leaf shakes in the wind, this is normal. But the more firmly the leaf can be attached to the branch, the groundedness of the trunk, the less likely it is to fall off. You will be moved by disturbances because you are human, and even we as spirit can be disturbed by events. But the deeper your roots, the more familiar you are with your centredness and your groundedness and your inner wisdom and knowing, the less you are likely to be shaken and stirred (like a cocktail)! You can be calm, centred, wise like a guide, a lighthouse, like the rock, steady. The steadiness will help you as well as help others. Developing that steadiness takes time, but it is achievable for everyone.

Bask in the sunshine of God and Spirit. Acknowledge that you are spirit in a human body experiencing your life. You do not have to retreat into a sanctuary to know your godliness. You can be stronger by staying in daily activity while remembering your godliness. And when doubt enters your mind, remember to pause and reconnect with who you truly are. Do not let the noise of the universe and the busyness of life allow you to forget the central rock that you are. You are Light, the image of God.

Be in the moment. Be present for the present; for the present is a gift. Do not get caught up in the past and the future. The past has been, and the future has yet to be. Enjoy now, the moment where you are right now, secure in your knowledge of who you truly are.

Honour yourself, your family, your friends, and your community, for this is your existence and your reality. Never allow yourself to be abused, for you are a child of God. And you have the right to say no. If someone is abusive to you, let them know and bless them. You always have the choice to walk away. And someone who is right for you at one time may not necessarily be right for you another time. And again, you have the right to change your mind. You have the right to walk away. It is not being selfish; it is taking care of your spirit. For you are a precious being, and you have a right to be here.

You came for a reason, a purpose, a learning. Remember the reason why you came, seek it. Ask Spirit for knowledge, insight and guidance. Ask us for help if you feel you need it, for we are always present and willing to help. But you must live your life and not be over-dependent. For life is a balance as we have said before. Yes, remember you are godlike, remember your spirit self but also remember you are leading a human being life. So be and do and laugh and play and learn.

Value yourselves. You are important and you do matter. Find your purpose and live your purpose. Find your light and remember your light, the light essence that you truly are. Embrace your essence, embrace your life. Give yourself hugs and be gentle with yourself, for life is not always easy. But the light does come on again, it is not always darkness. Like night and day, there can be times when you retreat, and there can be times when you are out in the world. Like summer and winter. Very often when life is difficult and you retreat, it is a time of learning, of developing. So, it is not negative, it simply is. Like grains of sand can irritate. The pearl grows with the irritation of the sand in the shell. So, irritation can be productive, can be useful. And you will become the smooth, lustrous pearl or shiny diamond with all the many facets of the diamond being polished by the grit of the sand, making the facet shinier, more perfect.

Allow your light to shine because you can take your light into darkness and illuminate the darkness for others. One light can make a difference to many. Be prepared to show your light. Stand up in your light. Be the beacon for others. So, it helps others come out of their darkness. It helps others remember their light. Stand up in your power. This is not arrogance. This is a willingness to help others, to guide others. If you have knowledge that can help others, allow that knowledge to shine forth. Be willing to help your brothers and sisters, your fellow travellers, whenever you can, as they will help you when you have dark times. Allow yourselves to be supported by us and supported by your family and friends. Have faith and trust. And stay in the moment, in the present.

Allow the rainbow of life, the many colours of the rainbow to be in your life. Each colour has a different vibration, a different frequency, and together they are perfect, and as individuals they are perfect. Like the rainbow, human beings are multiple personalities, colours, types, religions, and faiths. And they can harmonise together to become a beautiful rainbow. Like a mountain, there are many paths up the mountain to the Godhead. Allow others to take the paths that seem appropriate for them, for each path is right as long as progress is made, and learning is achieved. Be generous with others and their beliefs and systems of being. For together you can be a true rainbow of harmony and balance, of wisdom and knowledge. And be at peace with yourself and those around you. Be willing to turn the other cheek where necessary, but as we have said, be willing also to stand your ground and not let yourselves be abused or hurt.

Aim for harmony in your life, and balance; and remember that you are God-like.

Be kind to yourself and others.

And Peace be with you.

Talk 11 – With Elaine

31 August 2020

'Ahlan wa Sahlan.' This is I, Abdullah, and I make you welcome, and I thank you for welcoming me. Today we talk about evolution, advancement, evolving, advancing, a movement of growth, of more education and learning. Earth was merely energy, a spec in the universe, then it grew and evolved into the planet that we know today, and life became possible. And lifeforms were present that have now evolved to homo sapiens for a human being. Life forces come and go, like the dinosaurs. Events happen and occur, which stop things from being, and then new growth is formed, new things evolve where some things continue on and survive the cataclysmic events. And all is balance, all is development, evolvement, evolution. Some species die, some species are rediscovered, and some species adapt to new conditions. Humans should adapt and evolve. You are no longer Stone Age cavemen, which in a way is a pity because when you were Stone Age cavemen you honoured nature. You watched nature, you watched the skies. You knew of seasons, of planet change, you were aware of your surroundings, and you worked with nature. A lot of that gift has been lost as you so call advance. In your development you have lost a connection that you used to have to nature, and it is your responsibility to relearn that connection and let it be so alongside your technologies. Again balance, evolving, learning, to honour both the art and the science of life. The being in body and being of spirit at the same time.

Evolution of the soul, the soul develops. It becomes nearer to God, becomes purer as it learns, as it advances along life's path, many paths. You come back from time to time to further learn lessons you can learn as human beings. Once those lessons are learnt you continue on further into the spiritual planes, further develop your spiritual awareness. Becoming more godlike, more perfect, more ennobled, more knowledgeable. For there is wisdom that you learn on Earth, and there are other wisdoms that you learn in spiritual form. For life is a continuing existence, either in physical form or in spiritual form. For you never cease to exist. You are energy and life is continuous. It is important that you learn to work alongside and with your brothers and sisters on this planet. Your brothers and sisters of many colours, ages, wisdoms, and countries. There needs to be respect for all forms of humanity. You need to remember that you are spirit in human form. Honour that spirit, learn to work as a spirit in human form. Do not be judgemental of others. As Christ said, "remove the plank in your own eye before you move the spec of dirt in your other neighbour's eye." Do not be so full of yourself that you believe that you have no spec or plank of your own that you need to work with. None of you are perfect. If you were, you would not be on planet Earth, and it is fine to be imperfect because, as beings you are perfect, working out how to be even more complete and whole. Imperfections are perfectly acceptable as long as you learn from them. Learning is the key. Being as a spirit in human form, advancing and learning should be your aim during your lifetime. Do no harm to others, do no harm to yourselves. Be loving towards yourselves and your neighbours and friends. Be gentle with yourselves. We repeat these messages again and again because so often they are missed, forgotten, or you become so busy being busy that you forget.

Treasure yourselves, cherish yourselves. Remember you are children of God, in God's likeness. Remember your spirit form, your spirit being, your spirit light. Show your light to the world, to your neighbours. Polish your light by working on yourself, taking time out to remember your light and strengthening your light, by your connection with Spirit.

Be of good cheer. Life is to be enjoyed, so allow yourselves as you lighten up within, to lighten up your load, your physical load, of heavy work, heaviness, depression. Look within so that you can gather strength and peace and harmony. Peace of mind as well as peace of spirit. The more you can be at peace within yourselves, the less disharmony and disease will be around. You will be less susceptible to illnesses and stresses because you will have the strength of knowledge within you. You will realise the acquisition of unnecessary objects does not bring you the harmony and the peace that you seek.

You came with nothing, and you will leave with nothing but your soul, your spirit, and that is enough. Ensure you have a home over your head, enough food and a safe place to live. And spend time learning and growing. Have sufficient to exist and exist comfortably.

Do not be envious of others. Possessions do not always bring happiness. As long as you are secure and have enough, this should suffice. God does not wish you to suffer. Enjoy your existence while you are here. It is but a short period of time in your life span as spirit. As we have said before, it is a school of learning, development, advancement, evolution, but it is not the be all and end all. Harmonise with your surroundings, harmonise within yourself.

Apply yourself to learning, to developing; to developing your spiritual aspect as well as your human aspect. Knowledge is important, education is important, playtime is important, and laughter is important. Laughter lightens up the soul. It is like an inner massage of the body. It brings joy as long as it is laughter, not at the expense of others or the hurt of others. To laugh with others is important. To support others and take care of them when you can is important.

And taking care of yourself is very valuable and needful, for you are in the image of God. There is only one of you. You are unique and valuable. You do fit into the jigsaw of life, but sometimes you have to find exactly where your place is in the jigsaw. And for that, listen to your void, for inspiration from God source, for inner knowing. Your inner voice and guidance can lead you along the right path and can also warn you when it is the wrong path. Be prepared to listen. Use everything to your advantage. Hurt no one, including yourself.

You are like fish in the ocean, swimming along. There are different groups of you, different fish. Some of you swim in isolation, some of you swim in schools of fish. Each travels along its own appropriate path. None are wrong; they simply are. And by the differences, you intermingle. You each have worth, you each have your own reason for being and just because you choose to be the isolatory shark or within the school of fish does not make you wrong. If it feels right and you're doing no harm to anyone, then it is probably the right path. What is right for you may not be right for your brother or sister.

As parents, encourage your children to explore safely. Encourage their individuality, promote their independence and interdependence. Watch them with pride as they grow and stand on their own two feet. Teach them right from wrong, teach them respect for themselves and for others. Remember you are the parents, and it is your role to guide them, and steer them the right way. But be aware that your right way may not be theirs. So, do the best that you can but allow them their freedom more and more as they grow older. Support them, love them, and encourage them. Whenever you can, use positive words for them, for they are just seeds and seedlings and can be bruised easily and damaged easily. So be soft with your words, be loving and gentle. As a gentle rain on the Earth encourages seedlings and plants to come forward, do not crush them with too heavy a rain. Nurture their spark, nurture their spirit. They have come to you as a gift; treasure the gift that they are. Be honoured that they have come to you, by choice, to learn from you. They have chosen you so do not let them down. Have respect for them and yourselves. Care for them and care for yourselves.

Be harmonious and grow along your path. As the world evolves, allow yourselves to evolve and learn and grow and advance.

Be at peace. Love yourselves. Amen, Shalom, Salaam.

Talk 12 – With Elaine and Georgie

7th September 2020

'Ahlan wa Sahlan.' It is I, Abdullah, here today being with you and thanking you for your presence, for your presence is a gift to us, allowing us to communicate with you.

Embracing, embracing yourselves, embracing others, embracing the world where you live. Embracing the rough with the smooth, allowing, nurturing. All things balance, like the scales of life. The negatives, the positives, the tipping of the scales and then the rebalancing. Like the Egyptians using the scales to judge one's life. One should aim for balance, for harmony. Encourage balance in the universe and have balance in the universe

Gathering knowledge and wisdom, reaching out for knowledge. Do not waste your time on Earth. Study and learn. Learn for your enjoyment. If you do not enjoy the studying you are doing, change the course of study. Find that which resonates with you. Different subjects will resonate with different people. Very often you will find a book calls out to you, jumps off a shelf to you. So, study what you are drawn to. Education is important, but it is to be enjoyed.

Learning for children is important, a grounding, but encourage exploration. And never forget that you too are children, so allow yourselves to also explore and investigate. Do not waste your time on this planet, for this is all about learning.

Your journeying through life, learning, exploring so that when you return to us, you can celebrate a life lived fully and not just wasted. Be of good cheer. Even lessons that are hard are lessons that will teach you and show you. When you come to us there will be recognition. You will meet souls that have gone before you. You will reflect upon the lessons you have learnt. You will come into the presence of your Elders, where you will be judged gently by them and yourselves. And then you will continue to learn, for life is endless, continuous like loops within loops. You have a loop of time here, and then you have a loop of time in spirit until you gradually advance and grow so that you have no need to keep returning to Earth or other planes of experience. Sometimes you wonder why you have to go through struggles. This is for your life learning, for if life were always easy, there would be no learning.

Life is a vibration, there are souls that you will vibrate with and there will be other souls that you find you have nothing in common with. For they are on their own journey, their own exploration, and it doesn't cross with yours. You will have more than enough lessons to learn during this lifetime. For when you come here you choose a lesson to learn, and the greatest celebration is if you return to spirit having learnt the lesson completely. That gives you satisfaction and it gives us satisfaction. For it is like taking a suitcase and travelling and having an exploration, a journey; and then coming back to us and telling us about your exploration, journey, lessons you have learnt; how it has helped your soul develop. For our aim is to become closer to the Godhead, become purer.

Lessons are not always easy, but there also can be great joy. Your job is to embrace all of it; the good, the bad, the positive, the negative; embrace all of it as a learning. So that the facet of your soul that you are polishing becomes more polished, more gleaming, more knowing, more complete, and you have many facets to your soul, so let your light shine.

Also, embrace the bad with the good, for it is all for your evolvement and harmony. There would be no point in coming to this planet to learn nothing. That is not why you are here. Education comes on many levels, both from school and learning and also from life and exposure to life. So, you see, you are learning from the time you are an infant to the time you are mature enough and ready to return home to us. Earth is like a classroom, with many rooms for learning. And as you evolve, you choose different journeys to go on, different levels of understanding. Be gentle with yourselves, for you are human in this lifetime as well as spirit, and the human life is not always easy, but if it were, then you would not learn.

So, embrace yourselves on this journey, be kind to yourself and be open to learning the lessons, to exploring the reason why you came here at this time.

That is your soul's responsibility, to remember why you chose to come here. And to learn to the best of your ability about life and living. Be good to yourselves and be good to others. Help others along your path as you will receive help from others also. Be harmonious with others and be harmonious with yourself. Harmony is like a tinkling of bells that sound a beautiful chord, harmonious vibrations. Be in a harmonious vibration as often as you can be. Be wise and enjoy your pathway through this life.

Treasure your journey, for it is unique to you, for your lessons are unique to you. Celebrate being here, learning and experiencing and living your life. Remember, there are no mistakes, simply learning. Embrace your life and be at peace within and without. Remember, we love you. Remember, you are children of God and this is your playground, your place of learning.

Amen, Shalom, Salaam.

Talk 13 – With Elaine and Georgie

14 September 2020

We do say alleluia and we praise you for doing this work with us. There is much trouble on this planet at this time, and the planet needs all the help it can receive; you are true helpers on this path. You are allowing us to speak and to encourage, and you are giving of your time. For this we are grateful. Be at peace, my children.

'Ahlan wa Sahlan.' This is Abdullah, and I am here also thanking you.

Harmonics, chords of music can be cordant or discordant. Notes are placed upon the page and from that comes sound. And the aim is to make sweet sound, but sometimes discordant sound comes along. The best that you can do is try to stay in that space of sweet sound and allow the discordant notes to pass by you. Staying in the centre of the sweet sound helps to avoid clashes and disharmonies, and discordant chords slip by and do not touch you as much.

Harmonious sounds, harmonious living, harmonious being, that is the aim. Avoid the sounds of disquiet whenever possible. We realise that you live on a planet full of noise, animosity, and disturbance, but there are also many places of love and harmony. We have talked before about staying centred, nurturing your space, nurturing your void. This helps keep you immune from the noise and the clashing. Step softly on the Earth. Try to allow your vibrations to be harmonious and gentle. We are always present, supporting and loving you. Turn to us for reassurance when you need it.

Keep away from the 'battlefield' whenever possible. You have a choice to participate or not. Remember, it is important to take care of your soul, your spirit. Remember the contentment of the cow in the field, chewing. Try to be more like the cow, serene, content, just being, chewing grass. Each field has a boundary, a fence, and this is used to keep the cow within the field. It can be used as a border, a boundary, and you can place a boundary around yourselves when need be. Remove yourself from the battlefield and place yourself safely like the cow. Try to maintain your contentment within yourself. Avoid those that vex you whenever possible. Try to keep yourself out of the storm and in the sunshine.

Be like the river trickling along, slipping easily over and around the rocks, flowing on. Moving away from the source of the river and moving towards the ocean of life. You may find yourself in an eddy going nowhere for a while, and then a rock may move, a pebble may shift, which then allows you to continue on the journey along the river of life. So, there are pools where you rest, and there can be whirlpools where you spin, but always the water continues on. You are like water, coming from source and returning to source, and having a journey along that path from source to source. Everyone's trip is different, everyone's travel is different, but we all start from source and come back to source. Other tributaries join your river flow to make the swell larger. So, you start from small beginnings, and as you travel you become bigger. Other tributaries join you and you continue on. Like life, you start as one, you join with others, and you travel on until you return to source. Try to go with the flow; try not to resist but see where the flow leads you.

Sometimes the flow is smooth, sometimes it is more turbulent.

The flow continues as you travel through life until you decide it is time to enter the ocean of spirit. Life is meant to be an adventure so do not stagnate. Put your feet into the flow and explore and expand as you learn. Release the sides of the bank and swim with the flow. Do not stay at the side of the bank in fear; plunge in and enjoy. Participate fully in life. When you come against resistance it is sometimes easier to swim to the side of the bank temporarily, to choose the gentle stream rather than the fierce torrent.

Whenever possible enjoy the journey, and when it rains, remember that the sunshine will come, for there is always change. Whenever possible, be in harmony with yourself and others. Remember your harmonious chord and allow others to chime as they wish. Some will be harmonious to you and others may not. Sometimes orchestras make wonderful music, and sometimes they make discordant music.

You always have choices. Some like the excitement of discordancy, and others find harmonics more peaceful. Find the way that you would like to be.

So, splash in the river, explore, and choose to be harmonic whenever you can.

Like the flower, allow yourselves to open petal by petal and allow your centre to be fully open to the sunshine and the gentle rain. Turn your face to the Sun. Never allow yourself to be crushed by a heavy foot.

Live your life fully and be in harmony with yourself and in those that are around you and look to us when you need.

Remember, you are never alone.

Whenever possible, be at peace.

Amen, Shalom, Salaam.

Talk 14 – With Georgie and Elaine

24th September 2020

ALL IS WELL.

Harmony is the sound of the universe. The universe exists because of harmonious vibration. And the space between the planets is as necessary as the planets themselves. And there is interconnectedness of everything in the universe. It is not a question of a planet being alone in blackness. All is connected. The universe is one with many facets. Waveforms undulate, spreading outwards. Time is linear. There is a timeline, curved, not always straight. There are ebbs and flows, like the tide, which is pulled and controlled by the moon. And the power of the planets in your universe have an effect on you. The Sun, the Moon, and the other planets, as does the energy of the Earth. Tune in to the energy of the Earth, and listen with your inner ear, for the harmony, the vibration and the sound that Earth can make.

Sit and tune in like a radio receiver. Tune into the frequency where you can hear your inner voice, the quiet voice of wisdom within you. Harmonise with that voice for it is your God essence, your wisdom, your knowing. It is your soul sending you information like a speaker and receiver where you receive information through a speaker, but the speaker is quiet and soft.

Do not listen to harsh sounds of judgement and criticism. Consider the source when you hear that. And if that criticism and judgement is coming from you, then remember to be gentle with yourself, for you are a God essence. A God and a Goddess travailing in this lifetime on planet Earth. Travelling and travailing, so be gentle with yourself. When you hear yourself being critical, just acknowledge and then let it go, realising that voice is not coming from your loving essence.

For God and soul and spirit is love, and you deserve to receive that, the wisdom, sound of love, the harmony of love. We speak here of the harmony of the essence of love, the universality of love. Love between people is good, but the love that comes from the universe is so much greater. The harmony between people reflects in a small way the harmony of the universal love.

It is like the 'highs' that you seek. When you seek a 'high', it touches on the essence of the harmony of universal love, which is what you seek, the 'feel good' factor.

And yet you can receive that same 'feeling good' essence by being quiet and going within and allowing your soul and spirit to speak to you in the quiet. Allow yourself time for self-nurture. For it is good to be on your own for a period of time each day. Where you can self-nurture, self-love and remember who you truly are. For you truly are an everlasting being that continues on through the aeons of time. Death is merely a transformation from one vibration to another; your essence never dies. You always learn, and the speed at which you learn is your choice. For you can choose to not learn and just to be. However, by learning and exploring, you grow in wisdom.

Care for yourselves and care for others. Caring for yourself enables you to care for others more easily. For when you feel full and whole, it is easy to give to others. When you feel drained, it is less easy. So, nurture yourselves well, not just your physical body, but your spirit and soul body as well.

Spend time in nature, pause and look at the sky, the clouds, the trees. Fill yourself up and be content, be full of harmony. And when you are in this state, it is so much easier to help others, to give to others. To assist your neighbour on the road you are both travelling through life.

Spend time with yourself so that you learn of your beauty, your inner beauty. Remember the essence of who you were when you arrived here, your openness, uncluttered by prejudice and hatred. An open, loving soul. Remember that childlike innocence, for there is nothing wrong with being childlike. It is good to play. Being childlike allows you to learn without so much limitation, for your mind is open, like a sponge, and you are open to the wonderment of life, and you ask 'why?'.

It is good to ask 'why?' because by so doing, you learn, and you are never too old to learn. You learn throughout your life, for otherwise, you become stale, rigid, and stuck. Be inquisitive, ask questions. Question everything. Challenge. Do not just take what you are told as gospel. Consider the source. Question but also accept if it feels right for you. If it feels a good harmonious vibration and if it makes sense to you, accept. So, do not be over-critical. Question, study, learn. What you can accept, accept. What you cannot accept, release.

Each one of you has your own wisdom, and each one of you has your own path. What is right for one is not necessarily right for another. So, listen to your harmony, listen to your inner voice, follow your instinct, your inner knowing and trust. Trust that if it feels correct and harmonious with your vibration, then it is probably correct for you. And remember, you can change the path if it ceases to feel correct. Never get stuck on a path that has sharp pebbles on it. Always look for the smooth path, for life is supposed to be enjoyed.

You have been given a gift of life. It is your responsibility to travel along life's path with as much enjoyment, harmony, peace, and love as you can. For these are enduring sensations that you will then carry with you when you transfer vibration from physical to spiritual.

For all you take with you is your spirit and your soul, so enrich those. Ensure you are comfortable as you live whenever possible. Sometimes some discomfort is for your learning, but if it causes too much distress, or too much dis-ease, then it might be time to change your path, so it becomes smoother, lighter brighter.

Harmony of your soul and spirit is important. Disharmony can lead to disease of the physical and the mental state, and it is not our wish for you to suffer.

It is our wish for you to choose paths that cause easement on your soul while you are learning. So that when you transition from body to full spirit, you can celebrate your experience of what you have learned, explored, and discovered. And you return to us full of success and joy of a life well spent.

So, remember the harmony of the universe. All seems disconnected, separate planets and blackness. However, it is all interconnected; each has its place, and so do you.

Learn well, play well, laugh and love. Be whole, be harmonious. Love one another, for you are all interconnected. You are all one. This is a lesson you need to learn, the unity of mankind. For you are all dear souls that will return home when the time is right.

We give you our blessings and our love. Peace be with you.

Talk 15 – With Elaine and Georgie

1st October 2020

Thank you, children, for being here. We welcome you and your gathering here. We are the Council of Twelve and we bid you a good day. You are much loved by us, and we hold you in the palm of our hands, and we walk with you, the three of you. It is I, Abdullah. 'Ahlan wa Sahlan' and I bring you my greeting.

Reverence. Hold yourself in reverence. You are taught to revere God. It is important that you also revere the God part of yourselves. Be of good spirit and be of good joy, for you are children of God, and you are brave in coming to planet Earth to learn and expand your knowledge, expand your wisdom. This is a brave enterprise for you to do, for it takes strength. There are no accidents. Coming together like this is no accident. This was indeed planned before you arrived, and the timing is perfect for there are no accidents.

Evolution of the soul. As worlds evolve so do you. You expand your wisdom, your knowledge. We are not just talking about the knowledge that you read in books and on computers. We are talking about the knowledge of the spirit, of your purpose, of your inner knowing. Becoming aware of who you truly are, all aspects of yourself, your spiritual and your physical and your mental self. Some of you will have travails and troubles on your path, and they will feel unpleasant at the time. However, there are lessons to be learnt with these travails, these troubles, and it is all part of the plan for your development. And these troubles are of your choosing. You have chosen these before you came. Because you had decided before you came to planet Earth on the subjects, the issues you wanted to learn about while you were here. Because you do not suffer when you are in spirit, in heaven, and through suffering, you gain wisdom. And you wonder why you suffer, and it sometimes takes a whole lifetime to learn why you suffered. We have talked about this before, but it is like a tapestry where all you see is the back part of the tapestry, the knots, the sticking out parts. It looks a mess. And sometimes it is only when you come back to us that you can see the front part of the tapestry, the beautiful picture, the whole developed complete journey. And without one part you cannot have a complete picture of your journey. So sometimes you have to be patient and not know the answer until you return to us. But sometimes, if you sit, as we ask you to, if you sit and go within your void, within yourself, sometimes you get the answer of what is going on and why you are suffering at this moment. So, seek within, allow the small quiet voice of your spirit to be heard. This will help you when the road is rough, when you stumble and fall. But you do get up again and that is where you have courage, to stand up again and continue on. For those of you that decide not to carry on, for those of you that decide to give up and come home early, there is no wrong. There is just the waste of an opportunity, for you have been given this gift of life, this time on Earth, to learn. We would encourage you to gather your strength, go within, ask why, and be prepared to stand up again and continue on the path.

Do not regret lost time. You have a present, your life, your being on Earth. Do not waste it.

There are no wrongs should you choose to come home early, but you may find that you are sad that you have wasted an opportunity.

So, learn to reach out and ask for help when needed. No one has to be strong all the time, for you are all gentle souls. Speak out and ask for help. Do not be ashamed to ask for help. You do not have to be strong all the time.

Being weak is also a lesson. Showing emotion and tears are part of being human. There are no failures judged by us. It is all learning. The only failure is not being gentle with yourself. For you are all brave souls being here on planet Earth and it is not always easy. It is not meant to always be easy, for then you would not learn.

Celebrate being alive, celebrate your gift, your present, even on the dark days. Be patient with yourselves, be kind to yourselves. Learn much on all levels, mentally, physically, emotionally, for that is all part of who you are. Celebrate the gift of living.

If you are in severe intolerable pain, we do not frown upon a choice you might make to come home early. We do not want you to suffer. We look forward to the day when all the world allows people to choose to come back home when their pain will not cease or when death is inevitable, for you should not have to suffer. That is not our intent. Society has chosen to put limits on the termination of life. However, society is learning, and eventually all of planet Earth will find it acceptable, to come home early when there is deep suffering going on that cannot be resolved.

The dark days do not last for a long time if it is more a mental rather than a physical suffering. Realise that there is light around you when it seems dark. Seek for that light, seek as we have said to the light within, for the voice within you. Be patient with yourselves, be gentle with yourselves. For sometimes it seems so cloudy that you do not feel you can carry on, but the cloudiness will fade and does fade. And part of the cloudiness is the journey that you have chosen for deep learning. Love yourself, be gentle with yourself. Reach out and ask for help, ask for support. You do not have to be strong all the time.

You are not alone; you are never alone. We are always with you, lifting you up when you are down. It is sometimes very hard to see us, but trust that we are with you, encouraging you, supporting you, helping you on your path. When days seem long and dark, try to remember to go within; and you will see the light of the Spirit that is around you. Observe, in small ways, how you are being helped. You may feel that it is a coincidence, not significant. But do not discard these coincidences because coincidences can also be Spirit assistance. Trust that the dark days will become lighter, brighter. Hold yourself gently, as we hold you in the palms of our hands. You always have the choice to turn away from us, but we will still be with you, even if you choose not to see. Remember, we are always with you. There are no accidents, and you are always welcomed home when the time is right.

You are never judged by us. We love you. We guide you. We assist you.

You are here to learn, to play. Learning can be hard; that is why there should be balance. Playing and learning. Allow your heart to be joy-filled, joyful. Enjoy your gift of life. Run with the wind, play in the Sun, dance in the rain. Be happy on Earth.

It is just a short part of your whole experience of living and being alive, as a soul, as a being.

You have experienced many 'plays'. This is just another 'play' where you learn.

There are no accidents, we say again. And this is on all

levels. You are not a mistake. You have the right to be here. You have chosen to be here. Learn and enjoy. And when you are down and discouraged, remember we are here with you. So, turn within, listen for that still small voice of your own wisdom, your spirit, your soul. Connect with the part of you that is eternal, for that is who you truly are, an eternal being.

This is just a moment in time where you are learning what you cannot learn when you are in Spirit, the hard knocks of life, as well as the joys of life. Remember the lesson you chose by going within. Trust your intuition; trust the inner knowing that you have. You have the right to be here. You deserve to be here. You have chosen to be here. Learn, enjoy, and be at peace.

Remember you are all one. Each on your individual path, yet one. For you are all eternal souls. Be harmonious with each other. Lay the weapons of war down and embrace each other. Be at peace with all, with everyone, with nature. Release hate, embrace peace, embrace love. Love humankind, love yourself. Do no harm to others and do no harm to yourself, for you are precious beings much loved by us.

Amen, Shalom, Salaam, Namaste.

Talk 16 – With Elaine and Georgie

5th October 2020

'Ahlan wa Sahlan.' It is I, Abdullah, along with the Council of Twelve, and we come in greeting.
    Faith. Have faith in yourselves. Trust that you are exactly where you are meant to be in this moment. Have faith that all is well, all is right, you are all right. You have faith that the sun will rise in the morning and set in the evening and that the moon will rise in the evening and set in the morning. Balance, harmony.
    When life becomes uncertain and difficulties arise, have faith and trust that all is perfect; all is as it should be.
    Eternity is a long time; it is forever and what occurs one day is but a blink of the eye. What seems catastrophic one day is negligible when looked at from eternity. There is often a reason behind the 'madness' of life. There is cause-and-effect. The River of Life runs, sometimes it is smooth, and sometimes it is turbulent, but it runs. Sometimes it is swift, sometimes it runs over pebbles and rocks, and sometimes it is slow, meandering, where nothing much seems to happen, but all of this is balance. And so, with life. Believe in yourselves, believe in us. Have faith and trust that all is well.
    The minutiae of life can sometimes seem overwhelming, you feel overwhelmed. And that is like when the river is rushing in a torrent. And then you become becalmed in the meandering river. Life is like that, rushing and meandering.

(There is a brief silence. Warm sun rays suddenly come out, and it feels like an energy shift.)

The Sun pours its energy out to you. It gives you warmth, and it warms the planet. Without it life would cease to exist. The Earth rotates so that you have day and night. There has always been change. Through all the aeons nothing is static; nothing remains the same. There are ebbs and flows, too much heat, too little heat. The swings and roundabouts of the climate has occurred for many, many years. Awareness of the changes is important. Correct what you can, make adjustments but realise also that there are natural swings and roundabouts of climatic change. Have faith that life continues. There will be no cataclysmic disruption. Being aware of what is needed and where man can change events.

Man needs to be responsible for their actions, and when we talk about man, this is generic for human being. Man needs to be responsible for their actions. Causing unnecessary pollution by thoughtless thinking is not a good way to act.

Never be so mercenary that you do not care for the planet because you are more interested in money, making a fortune, profits.

The first thing that must be considered is, 'Is my action causing harm?' Consider the needs of many; consider the needs of the planet and the animal kingdom, and the mineral kingdom. Do no harm to yourselves and to others and to the animal and mineral kingdoms. Be considerate of others and all life forms.

Realise that when you harm others you harm yourself.

Know that you will have to be accountable for your actions. Be able to stand with pride about your actions. Stop when you know you are creating harm.

Nothing causes greater damage to one's soul than

deliberately harming others, whatever the reason.

Lay down your weapons of war. Lay down your poisonous chemicals.

Find other ways to communicate, other actions that do no harm.

Remember that nature nurtures you, so do not harm nature, for you simply harm yourselves. You poison the Earth, and you poison the crops that you then eat, thus poisoning yourselves. Consider your actions from all aspects. Do no harm to anyone or anything.

Bask in the rays of the warm sun, bask in the peace of the planet.

Cease military action for there is no need. Power and gain at the expense of others is nothing. Be harmonious with your actions.

Think what effect your action will have on yourself, on your brothers and sisters, on the Earth. Cease harming others, for it simply stains the lightness of your soul.

Be accountable for your actions, be responsible for your actions.

Remember your true essence. Your true essence is one of love, of harmony. Remember.

Recall the innocence of babies, their open, loving, harmonious spirit. You all were once that. And now that you have knowledge use it wisely and kindly.

Remember where you came from and remember where you go back to.

Cease terrorizing other people, cease the battles.

Focus on harmony of living, kindness, and gentleness.

Be proud of your actions, so that when you come back to us you have nothing to regret. Do nothing that stains your soul because you are always accountable for your actions.

Be able to stand with pride and humility; and gratefulness for having been given the gift of life. Be at one with yourself so that you can be at one with others.

(Long pause between each of the next statements.)

Be at peace with yourself so you can be at peace with others…

Keep your hand open in friendship, not clenched in a fist…

Be in harmony with your life…

Let a peaceful resonance run through your life…

Harmonise with yourself and harmonise with others…

Let your 'light' shine, your godlike essence shine…

Greet others with an open hand, love yourself and love others…

'Auf Wiedersehen' (until we meet again).

Talk 17 – With Elaine and Georgie

12th October 2020

It is in harmony that we come, the Council of Twelve and Abdullah. We come in harmony and greeting. Harmonising with yourself on all parts, physically, emotionally, spiritually, mentally; and harmonising with others and their harmony, their vibration.

We encourage peace. Peace and love are the most harmonious of vibrations. Love is a word that is used on so many levels, and sadly it has been misused on so many levels. Misused so that it has become less important than it is. It is seen as a physical as well as an emotional act. There are so many levels of love, and the most important one is Divine Love. Love of self, love of others, love of the universe. Being in a state of love and harmony so that you can be loving to others, just by your presence.

Love with a capital LOVE. Love from the Source. Sit every day so that you feel the Source of Love. For when you are in the state of love, you cannot create harm; you can only create peace, love and harmony. Yes, we encourage people to fall in love, to be in love with others; but it is equally important to be in love with yourself. This is not a state of arrogance. There is enough difficulty going through life, so loving oneself is very important, but the most important thing is the love of your spirit. And being in touch with the Divine Love of God of the universe.

Change occurs for many reasons. There is a saying that there is nothing more constant than change. We have talked before about the ebbs and flows of life. Sometimes change seems to be catastrophic, and yet looked at from a distance or with hindsight, it can seem the most perfect thing to have occurred. If you never had change, life could be very boring. If you always stayed in the same house where you were born and never left it and then died, you would have had an experience, but it would be somewhat limited.

Changing jobs and changing activities all add to the experience of life.

Sometimes you need to let go of friends who hinder your change, your growth, and that is a loss. But if they are being negative around your changes because they can't cope with them, then you need to take care of yourself and move on. You can outgrow other people, and they can choose to come with you or not, so there is change. Change is inevitable; it is part of life. Change can also mean growth. Never be scared of change. Some people get stuck with familiarity and refuse to move on, to grow, to learn.

So, see change as a challenge. Be excited for the unknown, for the adventure that is about to come. Dance in the light of change, do not be in fear. You came here to learn, to explore, expand, and this necessitates change at times. Neither be too restless. Do not seek change for change's sake, for grounding and developing roots is also good. If you are too restless, you are like a rolling stone which gathers no moss, no depth, no deep experience, for you are too busy rolling along.

When you experience change and feel shaky, go within, go into that void that we have talked about. Listen for the inner voice to see what we are trying to tell you, and how we are trying to reassure you.

Divine Love is loving people, nature, animals, and yourself. Try to feel secure in the middle of change. And take everything moment by moment; for even as the hands of a clock move, that is change. Time changes, seasons change, everything is change. Your growth from baby to adult to older is all change. Go with the flow, go with the stream, the river of life. Allow the meandering, allow the exploring. It is all part of your path, unclear at times, clear at others.

When you see the clouds in the sky and the storms, realise that above this level of clouds and storms there is blue sky and sunshine. Hidden from view for the current moment, but it is there as a constant. So are we in spirit; we are here with you always. Reach out and commune with us to help you feel more secure.

Maybe what you had was, in fact, rubbish, but you were comfortable with that rubbish. This is just an analogy. The rubbish made you feel warm and cosy, familiar, so you stayed there. There may be something even better for you, but sometimes you have to release the rubbish to be able to travel to the better. And that can sometimes involve risk as you let go of the rubbish and move towards the better. And sometimes this is forced upon you. In time you may look back and realise that the better was better than the rubbish, but this can take time.

There can be profound changes as you have experienced over these last months (Covid-19). Profound changes as to how you are living and being. On the one hand, you have the inconvenience of disruption, yet on the other hand you have a cleaner climate, fresher air, and less pollution. So it is like a scale, balancing the scales. Sometimes the scales tip quickly and sometimes slowly.

Have trust that all will be well, despite the disturbance, the fear, the risk. And if you find it is not so, then choose again. You have the right to be allowed to change. The decision made in one year may not be the right decision the following year. Do not allow yourselves to get stuck. Some habits are good, others are not. Allow yourselves to be fluid, to be prepared to move. And staying is also good if it seems right for you during that time.

One constant is yourself, your body, your spirit, and your soul during your lifetime. So, build your knowing, build your centre. Become strong within. Become familiar with your spiritual self so that you become the rock. So, you are a rock, and you are a river.

You are a spiritual being and a physical being. You will eventually lose your body, but your spirit and your soul are constant; you will go on forever.

So do not fear death. It is simply dropping an overcoat that you have worn for a season. So, with death you release the overcoat and come back to us, the true essence of your spirit and soul.

Realise that Heaven or Nirvana is here on Earth now. You do not have to wait to die to become spiritual; you *are* spiritual. You are spiritual beings living a physical life. Remember that.

That is why Divine Love is so important, because that is what you will experience when you are with us. All-encompassing love, peace, and harmony. But having that all the time can be boring also. So that is why you choose to manifest a body and become present on Earth to explore, experience, feel discomfort and feel joy, feel the extremes, and learn about balance. Take care of your overcoat for it carries your soul, your spirit. Do not abuse it, for as we have said before, it is a gift that you have been given, living on Earth. Enjoy your gift whenever possible. Be present in each and every moment of your life.

Whenever you can, enjoy your experiences, for they are all learning about life.

And you will return to us, to the Divine Love. Enjoy your journey.

Namaste. Go in Peace, Live in Peace, Be at Peace, Salaam.

Talk 18 – By myself

19th October 2020

Greetings, little one. We know that makes you laugh (I am large). We are the Council of Twelve and we thank you for working with us. 'Ahlan wa Sahlan.' It is I, Abdullah, and I come with greetings this day.

I want to talk about evolution and evolvement. Trappings of life can be so illusionary. One craves the trappings, the cars, the fine clothes, the jewellery, the fancy holidays, but this does not bring happiness. This does not bring permanent happiness; it brings temporary happiness and contentment. But this feeling is transitory and then you seek for something else, something bigger, larger. More and more and more, and it is never enough. There is always something else you yearn for when, in fact, you are really yearning for soul contentment. A feeling of peace and harmony, inner contentment, a feeling of 'fullness' within, contentment within. Being at peace within, being in a state of peace, being peaceful. If you are in this state of peacefulness, you cease to yearn so much for material goods because you are happy within yourself. Content, not yearning so much for something and trying to fill that something with material goods. Even those you call 'stars' oftentimes find discontentment because it's never enough. They try to rise to the top, and when they get to the top they fear they might fall off, so there is a sense of impermanence.

Inner harmony and peace give you a sense of permanence; it

gives you a sense of belonging, a 'right' sense. Peace is such a simple word and yet is so elusive.

The one thing that you are noticing during this pandemic is an aloneness. You miss the hugs, the endearments if you live on your own. Reach out if you can to help others. By so doing, you ease their loneliness, and you also ease yours. Reaching out to help, your brotherhood of man, your neighbour, your friend. Reach out and say hello. Also remember you can 'hug' yourself by being kind to yourself, by nurturing yourself in little ways. Do not be too hard on yourself, do not beat yourselves up. Life is hard enough without you doing that in addition. See where you can make a difference, be it ever so small. Shine your light in a dark corner and help illuminate someone else's life with a friendly word, a friendly greeting, or a wave through a window. A smile at a stranger as you walk on the street. You can always smile with your eyes as if you were smiling at a cat. People sense your energy, and they know when you are greeting them from behind a mask.

Be of good cheer; this will not last forever. And when it ceases to be so strident, so in your face, remember the benefits you have gained, and the universe has gained. The improved air quality, the cleaner streams, less pollution, warmth towards neighbours that you did not know before, communities formed by the Internet. Less rushing and more time to contemplate. These are all benefits. Remember to go within, into your 'void', your 'emptiness' and listen for our quiet guidance in little subtle ways; through your intuition, your knowing, words you may hear. Do not discount them as meaningless, coincidence, nothingness. These are the quiet words from God and Spirit to encourage you on your way, on your path.

Especially at this time, reach out to teenagers and youth who are struggling with the uncertainty of their life's path and the meaning of life. Reach out and encourage communication with these spirits, for they are suffering, and too many of them want to end it. Try not to over-listen to press, to negative news; limit your exposure to that. Go for a walk, breathe in the air, stand in the light of the day, even when the sun is not shining. Being outside for a little while is good for the body and the soul.

Make your surroundings more harmonious and clean up the messes. For you will live in more peace and harmony if your surroundings are more harmonious wherever possible. Each home should be a sanctuary, a place where you feel blessed and safe. So, whereas your body houses your spirit, so does your house 'house'; your body. Give thanks that you are surrounded by a building. Make it as harmonious and homelike as you can.

And for those of you that have no home, trust that you will be cared for, looked after by society, a society that cares and nurtures the less well off; the downtrodden, the homeless, the hopeless. And for those that choose to be free, without a home, that is their choice when they choose not to go into shelters. Make room in your society for those who are less well-off and count your blessings because there but for the grace of God, that could be you. So do not be arrogant in your good fortune. Be thankful and grateful and realise how lucky you are to have had good opportunities.

Clean up the messes, clean up the trash, clean up your trash, your messes. Make amends to people whenever possible if you have hurt them. Even writing a letter, even if you're not able to send it, the act of writing is an energetic release for the good. You will feel lighter and brighter by asking forgiveness when you have done wrong, and we all do wrong, for we are human. This is where we come, to planet Earth, to do wrong at times, to learn from our mistakes.

Whenever possible, say that you are sorry if you have hurt another. Make amends, release resentments, and release the anger you hold within, for it only harms you. It gnaws away, like an inner worm, when you hold onto the inner anger. You may be in the right; however, holding onto the anger is like a festering sore that only hurts you, not the other. So, forgive the other if they have hurt you and try to let it go, knowing that karma exists. And if they have done wrong to you, they will have to repay on some level. Let go and let God sort out the issue. Trust that things unfold as they should. Sometimes the 'fixing' is done at a later date and not by you. You have simply set the issue in motion. So, whenever you can, make amends if you need to. Release the anger you hold onto, for it does not serve you. It leads to higher pressure in the blood, resentment, bitterness, stomach ulcers, and dis-ease.

Try to live the best life that you can, day by day. Forgive yourself when you make a mistake; rectify the mistake whenever possible. Seek forgiveness whenever appropriate and then allow yourself to move forward, for tomorrow is a new day, and there are many tomorrows.

Do what you can to create peace in this world, 'mending fences' with your neighbour, reaching out to mend fences within your community, and reaching out to help within your community. Taking care of yourself and also helping to take care of others, monetarily or tangibly.

Clean up your house, your home, clean up your community. It does make a difference, even though you may not see it from day to day. If each community cleaned up, this world would be a much better place.

As we have said before, do no harm. Turn the other cheek if

necessary. You will be the bigger person for it, the better person for it.

Speak your truth.

Be in a state of peacefulness every day whenever possible.

Amen, Namaste, Shalom, Salaam.

Talk 19 – With Elaine and Georgie

26th October 2020

'Ahlan wa Sahlan.' It is I, Abdullah, coming to greet you this day, and we, the Council of Twelve, likewise are here. Welcome our children, and we give thanks for your presence.

Absolution. Absolve yourselves of anything that you think you've done wrong. Forgive yourselves, be kind to yourselves, for making mistakes is human. So, absolve yourselves if you feel you have done wrong. Give yourselves permission to be human, for that is what you are, and that is why you are here.

Forgiveness of yourselves and forgiveness of others. Try not to judge too harshly your fellow brethren that walk with you, for you are all children no matter what age. You are all children trying to do the best you can and stumbling every now and again is just human. So be gentle with yourselves and with others. For each of you have a path upon which you are travelling, and you cannot understand another's path fully, for they are sorting out their issues while you sort out yours. What may seem obvious to you may not be obvious to them. So do not be too harsh on others.

Realise that each one of you is a diamond in the rough. Each one of you is trying to shine your diamond. Polish the facet of the diamond that you are, that your soul is. Your soul is multifaceted, you are multifaceted, and when you come to Earth, you are focusing on a facet of your character, of your essence, and working out that facet. So whether you have been over-dependent in the past and the learning is independence; whether you have been too independent in the past and need to learn how to blend with others, it is all progress. Trying to become whole, trying to become pure spirit, as pure as you can. So, that you become more like the Godhead, you become closer to perfection, to the Godhead. To the universal harmony of life, of being.

You enrolled in the school of life when you arrived here. And gradually, through your lives, you develop. The art of living is discovering and re-remembering that you are spirit, first and foremost. Not waiting until you come back to us to discover and remember that. Becoming actively aware that you are spirit living in the human body.

When you see yourselves doing wrong, catch yourselves in that moment and readjust; so that you stay on a more direct course during your sojourn of life. So that when you return to us you can rejoice in having achieved the goal, the aim of why you came. So that you can say, "I have learnt what I came for," and then you can celebrate with us on your return. You then may choose, at a later date, to return again to Earth to polish a different facet, a different aspect of yourselves.

Once you are whole and can no longer learn lessons that you learn on Earth, then you progress further. Discovering new levels of being. Developing your skills, being of service, even within spirit: for even in spirit, you continue to learn and progress.

There are schools of learning, centres of learning, many communities, many existences, and you can choose which path you want to take. You will meet up with loved ones, ones who have gone before you, and there will be much joy and much happiness. You will remix with those that you love, and they will greet you and show you the way. They will take you and show you the various places, the schools of learning. Colours are more vibrant, and you will feel lightness within yourselves. You will feel peace and love.

And like a butterfly, you may choose to go here and there, flutter from place to place, exploring, creating, or you may choose to stay in one place to learn and grow. Similar to Earth, where some of you choose to be in one place, and others of you choose to be like butterflies, travelling from place to place. All is learning. You have many opportunities on planet Earth for learning, growing, and progressing, and you can choose to be in one place, or you can choose to be like the butterfly; all is development.

Even making mistakes is development because by your mistakes you learn. The depth of your soul progresses, the multilevel, multi-layering of your soul continues to develop; your character deepens.

And you learn wisdom through experience, positive and negative.

Music can be heard as one note or a chord. The one note is more simplistic, and the chord is more evolved. And so, it is with your soul and your learning. You can choose to learn on a light, simple level, with few complications during your life, or you can choose to have what you would term a difficult life. A multilevel chord, like a chord with many aspects and notes, is more complex; and this deepens your experience. So, you learn on many levels, more complicated. Some of you choose to be like the single note, and some of you choose to be the chord, depending on your life learning. And each is right, for each is on their own path.

So, when you have children, realise they are diamonds in the rough. They have come to learn their life lessons. You are sometimes surprised that when you have children, they are so different. That is because they have their own lessons to learn. And they have chosen you to be their guardians when they are young because your life's circumstances help them with their lessons.

So do not crush the sparkle out of the diamonds that you have. Help them polish their sparkle so that they can walk forward. And not be crushed or damaged by being handled too heavily. Nurture their inquisitive minds, their explorations. Never shame them. Because by shaming them you dampen their light, their sparkle. You bruise their souls. You have been given a gift when you receive a child; nurture that gift with love, for you have been honoured to receive a spirit at the beginning of its path on Earth.

Likewise, treasure yourselves, for you are also children in grown-up bodies. Because you are so young, because you are still learning, and remember it is all right to make mistakes because it is a learning experience. So do not wrong yourself for it; absolve yourself and realise that you are simply learning.

For that is what life is, a learning experience, and then you come home to us to continue learning. But the lessons are harder on planet Earth. There are some lessons you can only learn by being on planet Earth; hence you choose to come here to help progress your soul; to polish your various facets. Try not to be rigid; allow yourselves to be fluid. Rigidity can cause a narrowness of life experience. Be open to exploring, do not resist change, for change is also learning. Do not be in fear, but step bravely forward on your path of learning, of exploring, experiencing, of living.

Be of good cheer, for we are with you on this path. We accompany you and watch over you.

But it is you that has to learn. By remembering that you are spirit, you will not feel so alone and lost, for there is indeed purpose in you being here.

And your purpose is to find your purpose, why you chose to come, and what you chose to learn.

And you can do this by communing with us, as we have said. Spending a little time each day, being with yourselves. Listening to the quiet voice within, the guidance, the intuition.

For we are here to help and assist, but we do not interfere.

Be open to asking us for assistance when you choose.

Auf Wiedersehen, Shalom, Salaam.

Talk 20 – With Georgie and Elaine

3rd November 2020

GUIDELINES FOR LIVING

Communion with Spirit, communion with the Godhead. You can commune with nature. You can commune without speaking just by being open and willing to blend. So, communing with Spirit and the energy of God is beneficial.

This energy makes one feel fulfilled, complete and at peace.

'Ahlan wa Sahlan.' It is I Abdullah, along with the Council of Twelve. We bring you our greetings, and we can commune with you each time we meet. Not only do we talk, but our energies are here with us, with you, giving you our blessings, our energy.

Communion is the Blessed Sacrament within a church service. But it is also our touching you, our being with you, blending, coming close. So, it is like the sanctity of a prayer

Nurture yourselves with this communion, feed yourselves with it, for it does indeed fill your soul by so doing.

(There is a different energy in the room, female. Saint Maria Magdalena de Pazzi, who has not been obviously talking since 2016. After this session, Georgie, who has been aware of a Nun around her since she joined us, 'saw' her just before I started speaking. Georgie asked her who she was and was told Saint Maria Magdalena de Pazzi.)

Communion with God is so important. Make it a rule to give

yourself time, which is so easily forgotten. (The word 'rule' is not negative; it is simply a reminder, a guide.) As normal as brushing your teeth, it becomes a habit, it becomes automatic, and you feel wrong if you have not completed sometime.

You will notice that there is a tendency for your day to go better when you have spent a little while nurturing your soul by communing with it and acknowledging your spiritual self.

For that is one of the main reasons for which you are here. To remember that you are spirit and learn with the wisdom of knowing that, rather than waiting until you return to us.

You will find your path easier with this awareness and taking the time. Make it a habit, for it is a good one and will benefit you in many ways.

You can make it a ritual and this ritual can be simple or complex; that is your choice.

The key is the communion with Spirit, your spirit and the spirit that surrounds you, and the Godhead. Come into contact with the divine love of the Godhead. The never-ending love, the constant love, love that is unconditional.

For you are a beautiful soul and are loved, completely, forever.

And you are having an experience being in the physical body. An experience that you chose before you came to the planet; and you learn, and you play, and you make mistakes. Your aim is to do no harm to others, to live in peace and be at peace, and create peace wherever you can. Peace and harmony and love.

Open your hearts, open your hands in greeting. Be aware of the many wonders that are here surrounding you. Seek for the positive in everything. Embrace yourself and embrace others. Be kind to one another.

Make your homes sanctuaries for you and your families; a

place of refuge and harmony where you can safely BE.

Life can be simple, and you can be like children, playing nicely together, sharing the toys in the sandpit. Giving with an open hand. Smiling at others, even if you do not know them.

Where there are troubled waters, try to smooth them. Make amends when you need to.

Play nice. Be a good friend.

Sometimes you have to let go. But there are no accidents and letting go of one thing allows a flow into you of another. So do not hold tight in fear.

Whenever possible, be in a state of love and harmony and trust. Trust all is well and that the sun shines after the storm.

Sometimes you ask why? Sometimes you will know, and sometimes you have to just trust. But there are no accidents. You will know later the answer to your 'why'.

Even during this difficult time (Covid-19), there is a reason amidst the chaos. The reason is not always clearly seen. Trust that there is a pattern which cannot always be seen clearly.

Be in the moment. Live your life fully. For you are not here for long, so try to enjoy the experience whenever possible. Make your life count.

Serve others whenever you can. But make sure you take care of yourselves, for you are precious beings, much loved by us.

Allow your menfolk to show emotions, to not always have to be strong. To commune with us, for this will lead to less troubled souls.

Take the time to tell those you love, that you love them. This is the best gift that you can give.

Be grateful for the things in your life. Having an attitude of gratitude will result in you having more things in your life.

Be thankful for your many blessings. And be full of love, as much as possible. The more you give, the more you get. Never be ashamed to let those you love know this.

Be kind. And walk gently on this Earth. Do no harm to yourselves or others. Be at peace.

Amen, Shalom, Salaam, Auf Wiedersehen, Namaste.

Talk 21 – With Elaine and Georgie

9th November 2020

Like the ticking of a clock, the heart beats from before we are born until the day we die. And the heart is a miracle. It constantly moves, pumping blood around us, but it is also an organ of feeling, for feeling emotion, for feeling love. That is how we connect with Spirit, how we resonate with others by our 'heart light'. Pay attention at times to your heart and your lungs, for they are life-giving, and they just work automatically. And you can choose to work automatically, to be an automaton, and just carry on each day, or you can choose to recognise your heart and the job it is doing, both on the physical and energetic level.

Your heart is your essence. When you feel lifted up in ecstasy, it is felt in your heart area. You can be illuminated in the moment with your spiritual connection, and you may feel it throughout your whole body, but chiefly it radiates in your heart area. And like the regular beating of the heart and the ticking of the clock, we as Spirit can always be present with you each day, each minute. And you can choose to be aware of us, and whether you are aware of us or not, we are always present, watching, and guiding.

Children of the Earth, pay attention to the multiple aspects of yourselves. Your physical aspect but also your mental, emotional, and spiritual aspects. Respect your bodies, be in love with your bodies, for they hold the essence of who you truly are.

You have a choice each day to focus on the negative or focus on the positive. Try whenever possible to focus on the positive. For by focusing on the negative you can bring yourselves even further down. So, you look downcast, you look down and you feel down. Whereas if you look up, you can feel more lifted up, more at peace, more in harmony with yourselves. Do not look too far forward for change can occur. Try to be as positive as you can in this moment, at this time, for this is where you are, right here and now.

Treat yourself like a rose, like a flower; be gentle with yourselves and your petals. Do not be unkind to yourselves.

For you have been given a gift, and that gift is being here on Earth, present. So live life to the full. Grab life with both hands and enjoy every moment. Do not take things for granted.

Cherish yourselves and cherish those around you. Cherish your families and your friends. And know that you can make a difference in your environment and in your surroundings.

Try to not rush through the day. Try to take moments here and there through the day where you stop and appreciate who you are and where you are.

Enjoy your health whenever possible. Do not take it for granted either. Appreciate your existence. Try to be true to yourselves. Speak your truth without causing harm.

Entertain the fact that you are here, a spirit embodied in a body. And sometimes, when you are not well and you wonder why, entertain the fact that maybe your illness, your un-wellness, is teaching you a lesson about yourself.

Sometimes the lesson is hard to understand. But sometimes you have to become unwell in order to stop and reflect and to heal.

Sometimes the lesson is dependence on others, giving them

the gift of allowing them to help you, to take care of you. To be able to nurture you and show you how much they love you. It is like a pause in the busyness of life. It forces you to stop and to give your body and mind time to recover. It shows you that you do not have to be always on your own.

But it would be nice to learn these lessons without having to become unwell. So do not be *so* busy all the time. It is a blend of being busy and also just being. Difficult times can increase your knowledge, your understanding and your wisdom. Like the boulder in the river, it breaks your journey and slows your journey for a while.

Do not use illness as a means to escape living life; for living life and maximising your life is so important.

Having been given the gift of life, use it to the full. And it comes with a rough and a smooth side, and sometimes you have to experience the rough to then appreciate the smooth. Be grateful for the smooth sides, for the blessings that you have.

Appreciate the gifts that you are given from friends and family, and good health. Laugh often and love much.

Have your eyes open so you see the beauty of the world. Stop and breathe and appreciate from time to time. Look into the sky, see the birds, how they adapt to weather conditions, to the wind. And when it becomes too windy, they pause and stop their flight. Take lessons from nature. Whenever possible, breathe in fresh air, walk in nature with eyes open and lungs full of fresh air.

Treasure your beating heart for it gives you life. Sometimes your heart will feel broken from events, but this too can be learning, and wisdom gained.

Recognise your heart light and the heart light in others. So that when you see another, you see the essence within them, for they too are a fellow spirit travelling their journey.

No one is your enemy in the natural plan. Ideally, you all harmonise, each living their own lives.

Try to learn to be at peace with each other. Lay down the weapons of war and embrace each other whenever possible.

Let this planet become one of harmony, love, and peace. Each one of you can make that happen by having it in your own environment as much as possible. And so, it spreads around the globe. Let it happen in your lifetime.

Focus on being in a state of peace every day. Things will irritate and annoy, but you can choose whether to stay in that state or return to the state of peace. It is up to you. You can make a difference in this world. Each one of you in turn.

Do not waste a moment in anger and rage. Try, whenever possible, to re-harmonise as soon as you can.

Hold love in your hearts. Let love be your essence, your choice, your state of being. For when in that state there can be no hate, no disharmony, no war, no battle.

Refuse to pick up arms. Stand for peace. Live in peace whenever you can.

Allow your heart to radiate peace and love, and joy.

Auf Wiedersehen, Namaste, Shalom, Salaam.

Talk 22 – With Elaine and Georgie

16th November 2020

AND WHAT IS DEATH?

It is merely a transition from this world to the next. Where you transfer from being spirit in the human body to coming to us without a physical body but a spiritual body. You are met and greeted by your friends and family, and you are made welcome. You travel to the part of the spirit world that suits you, where you belong, where your friends have gathered.

You are given time to heal and recover from the transition. And then there is an accounting where you recount what you have done on Earth. And you are listened to, observed, and advised. Then you transfer to your home base where you will meet up with your Soul Group, those that travel with you, that you have travelled together with for a long time, aeons of time.

You choose to come to planet Earth together as a group, some of you in your Soul Group and choose to learn lessons. You choose where you are born, your parents, and the outline of what you have chosen to learn. However, much freedom is given to you; you always have freedom of choice. You have activities and events along the way and learnings. And then you come back to us, transitioning again, dropping the human body, and returning to Spirit where you continue to learn. For life is an eternal learning process, a growth process.

Life is eternal. Your energy and essence are eternal.

It is simply that from the Earth point of view, you pass away, and you leave the Earth. Those that are here on Earth grieve, and those that are in heaven rejoice at your coming back home to them.

Life and death and then birth and life; it is all balance.

The soul that is leaving, once it has left the body, experiences a lot of freedom, enjoyment, and release from the heavy tensions of the Earth. There is a lightness of being, and they rejoice in the abundance of love and peace and harmony that they return to.

The transitioning from life to death sometimes can be hard, but the actual event of passing from body to spirit is easily done and smooth. The spirit is very often met by loved ones before they even transition. They are accompanied on the journey, the journey home, by those they love.

There is lightness where we are. There is a sun that shines, a sun that creates no harm. A lightness, a brightness, a warmth, and all is peace, harmony and abundance. There can be playtime and relaxation time, and should you choose, there is learning time. There are orchestras of music that are so beautiful. And Halls of Learning where you can look at where you have been in the past and where you are in the present.

You have a choice as to what you wish to do while you are in Spirit, for there are hospitals and schools of learning and creativity, an abundance of opportunities. It is simply your choice as to what you wish to do.

And in time you advance further. You progress along the evolution stages of spirit from one level to the next until you reach Nirvana, where you are filled with the God-force and peace and harmony.

And there is always work to do should you choose to do it, for you have freedom in the land of Spirit as you do on planet

Earth. The path is easier in the land of Spirit. There is a radiance, an essence of peace and love.

So do not fear death, for it is simply a passing from one room into another, transiting from one place to another.

Do not allow the fear of death and dying to impact how you live and learn. Live your life fully. For, as we have said before, it is a gift to be enjoyed fully. Take every opportunity; use everything to your advantage.

Your family can be part of your Soul Group, and you choose to travel together and come together as a group here on Earth to learn your lessons. You may come at one time as the mother or the father or the child. And there is a 'knowing' when you meet the members of your soul group. You recognise something about them. And sometimes the recognition is preordained, arranged before you come; there may be a symbol.

Sometimes when there is difficulty within the family, it is because the members of the family are teaching the others. You role-play to help each other learn the lessons you have come for. But this should not be a painful experience; simply a learning for all concerned. And the many souls that you meet along your path can each teach each other.

There are no accidents. There can be mistakes and errors, but then those errors and mistakes can also be learning tools and learning experiences.

Life is not meant to be one long journey of pleasure, for then you would not learn, and you are here to learn amidst the play. For God wants you to enjoy being here but being here is not always a playground.

Look back along your path and see where you had difficult times. Did they not teach you something? Something which you would not have learnt had it been smooth sailing? Like the sailor on a ship; on a boat. During stormy times, the sailor uses extra skills and learns how to work with nature.

And there is pride and achievement through difficulties. Take pride in the lessons that you learn, for it is not always easy, but it is part of your pathway, your learning, and your schooling on planet Earth. And when it is time, you come home to us.

And those of you that remain, try not to over-grieve. Continue on with your life journey. Do not become stuck in grief, for that negates your learning. Remember that those you lose are still often around you in spirit, so all is not lost. They are amongst your helpers. So, remember that you will meet up again when it is your turn to pass over to Spirit.

Treasure the gold... the gold of being alive. Grab the gold with both hands and enjoy the treasure, moment to moment. You have earned the right to be here.

You have been given the gift (of life). Treasure it, value it, enjoy it with all its ups and downs, knowing that it is just a part of your existence, your experience.

For you continue forever as a light being of energy. A soul of wisdom continuing to gain wisdom, learning, evolving, coming closer to the Godhead over time. And time is endless.

Existence IS. And you will always exist.

So do not fear death. It is simply an ending of one chapter and the beginning of another.

Fear not. And enjoy the fullness of life while you are here.

Amen, Shalom, Salaam, Auf Wiedersehen.

Talk 23 – With Georgie and Elaine

23rd November 2020

ILLUMINATION

We give you greetings, and we are the Council of Twelve. We are pleased to be with you today. We come in harmony and blessing. We give you our blessings and our love.

(Energy shifts to female... Saint Maria Magdalena de Pazzi?)

Children, you are indeed blessed. We bring you our blessings, our love, and our thanks for being here, willing to meet with us.

Illumination: Light shines on the universe, on the Earth like a soothing balm. Each one of you is like a light, a sparkling light, and we know you by your light. We recognise you by your light, spirit light, your soul light.

You are well known to us and well-loved. We follow your progress with interest, and we observe from afar. We keep an eye upon you, yet we do not interfere unless you ask.

'Knock and the door shall be opened'... So, when you seek help, ask, and we will be there, assisting you on many levels. We may be seen or unseen; you may be aware of us by a sense, a smell, intuition, an 'aha' moment, or our presence may be reflected by what somebody says to you.

We will not let you stumble. We will lift you up; we will give you wings to lift yourselves up with. You are protected, yet you have to experience in order to learn. If it is not your time to come back to us, we will assist in stopping you from stumbling.

Illumination is also about light being shone upon you, and the light is there within you, but you have to seek it out. It is present in the void, in that space within you. That is why we encourage you to spend time each day looking within, being aware of within you. For the answers are there, not with some guru. YOU have the information if you seek within.

But the information is not always obvious; it can be subtle. Give time for that 'still small voice' within you, for that is your illumination; that is your Light.

When you have a searchlight, there is a beam, and the beam focuses on a point and illuminates that point. That point is available for you, within you. So, you can travel to many lands, seek from many wise people, but your own personal issues are more understandable if you go within you to that still small voice. This takes patience and persistence. You may get an answer one day but not another. You may get an answer but not realise that it is an answer. It may not be the answer that you wish. Sometimes what you wish for is not necessarily in your best interest, your best lesson.

Realise we work with you for your best interest, for what makes you grow and learn. We try to illuminate your path as much as possible. And sometimes you choose to look in the other direction. Realise that you are enough, that you do have the resource within you, within that space which you try to avoid.

Do not assume false posture; be comfortable. Have a time of your choosing each day and allow us to teach you and show you. Answers may also come in the dream state, for you also learn while you are asleep. Learn from many sources, friends, family, and situations.

When you question and feel lost, come back to us. Come back to sitting in the quietness, for the quietness can be full of richness. And yet most of you are not trained to sit in the quiet, the silence. The quiet can make you uncomfortable, so you keep busy with activities and sounds.

You can also have quiet time when you walk, ideally in nature, in the countryside. But you can also make a walk a sacred experience if you choose to focus on that, even sitting in your car quietly, making sure it is not moving! If you choose to focus on it, even walking into a shop, if you are aware and in a state of mindfulness, you can make that experience meaningful.

People that you meet, that you smile at, strangers, friends; each of them can reflect back to you the soul that they are and the soul that you are.

Try to become conscious in your activities so that you see the spiritual aspects, the godlike occasions. Helping someone who stumbles and assisting them can be a godlike occasion, where you are being of service to others.

Try to become aware of who you are and what you are. Practice making an activity a spiritual event. Seek for the sacredness within an occasion, a moment. Give the spiritual aspect of yourselves an exercise, a chance to be truly active in your busy, practical day.

These experiences will enrich you, will bring joy to your heart and fulfil you. So, let the illumined soul that you are, shine forth; show others the way by your example, by your light, by your goodness

Look into the stars in the sky at night and observe the illumination of the moon and stars whenever you can. It is all part of your world, the universe, likewise with the Sun. Enjoy the rays of the sun and its illumination, but do not stare directly at the orb. You can observe the rays and you can feel the heat, the warmth of the sun's rays.

Be an observer of where you are; do not take it for granted. Whether you are in a city or the country, there are things to observe, people to see, and people to help.

Allow the God force within you to show, just by being the way you are. Because every moment has the opportunity of being sacred should you choose to view it in that way.

So, come to us in your meditations and reflections... for illumination.

Illuminate others with your love, compassion and understanding. Observe the many beautiful events that occur on a daily basis when seen with an open knowing eye.

Seek for the positive in everything, minimise the negativity that is around you, that you hear about, read about. Whenever possible, focus on the positive, absorb that and our illumination and the illumination of other positive beings, events, and circumstances.

Whenever possible, be happy, filled with joy and laughter.

Love your animals as they love you, unconditionally.

Love your life whenever possible. You have been given an opportunity to be a physical being, experiencing and learning.

Enjoy the experience and learn. For life is about experimentation, exploring, and learning.

Remember to ask us for support when you feel the need, for we are always nearby, watching over you with love, unconditional love.

We illuminate you with our love. Bask in it, for it is always there.

All you have to do is turn within to feel it and to be reassured by it. Let us help you along your path whenever you choose.

Namaste, Shalom, Salaam.

Talk 24 – With Elaine and Georgie

30th November 2020

Greetings, our children. We are the Council of Twelve and we come here today to blend with you and talk with you.

Life is a mystery and there are many mysteries in the universe. The Black Holes, the vortexes of energy, the other universes that exist but are not seen. They may be not seen but they are present, as is the substance of the universe, the matrix of energy, the cobweb, spiders web of life; the inter-threading of substance between the planets surrounding you.

If you have the eyes to see, you can see auras, ever-changing energies, and bandwidths of colour that surround you, reflecting the energetic being that you are. A few of you have this gift, this ability to see the energetic patterns and changes. However, there is no point in seeing these changes unless they have meaning for you and signify something. Very often you feel the energy, the aura. You feel when someone is withdrawn energetically or when someone is expanded energetically. You may be irritated by some of the energetics of people, and you may be attracted to the energetics of others. As you are energy so you can react and be attracted to other energies.

'Resistance is futile'. You are energy and you cannot change this fact. Your whole body is an energetic force. There is interconnectedness within the organs of the body. And there is likewise an interconnectedness with the spirit part of you as well as the physical part of you, for you are much more than a physical being. The physical being is complex. A reaction in one part of the body can cause another reaction in another part of the body. Ideally, the body harmonises, but there are times when there is discord and disharmony within the body. Stress can cause some of this disharmony. Too much excess of stress causes distress, dis-ease and this can lead to illness. When there is too much stress, the blood pressure can increase, the heart rate can increase, and this can lead to complications. Sometimes diet is wrong, choices are wrong, and too much of one substance can cause complications in the body. But we have said before, it is important to nurture the body and take care of it. Make sure that you get to sleep and rest and play as well as work. For not only does your body need this for health, but also you as spirit need this for health. Too much of one thing can cause damage if taken in excess or done in excess.

The art of balance must be learnt in order to have a healthy, productive life. For it is all about play as well as work, rest as well as labour. Your body recreates itself in infinitesimal ways. Skin is rebuilt, bones are reshaped, and blood is rebuilt from time to time. So, there is always an ability to improve and heal. However, sometimes the damage has already been established and cannot be undone; but this is not always the way. Healing can occur on many levels; spiritually, emotionally, physically, and mentally.

Be compassionate to those who suffer mentally, for this is often a chemical imbalance. A dis-ease of the body structure and the brain matter.

Be patient with those who are not like yourselves, for everyone is different. Each has their lesson to learn, and it may come physically, mentally, emotionally, and spiritually.

You are all universal beings. You as energy exist continually. So, you are universal energetic beings.

Lightning can be different. Sheet lightning, forked lightning; it is all lightning, but it is different. And the power in lightning is tremendous. It also is an energetic force. Like you, an energetic force. And there can be lightning in the skies and storms and turbulence. And there can also be smoothness and lightness, as with your lives. The storms do pass. The storms can cause changes, can clear the air, the atmosphere.

Likewise, storms in your life can create a clearance. In the midst of the storm it can be difficult; but after the storm, is over, there is a clearness in the air, a washing away of dirt.

Sometimes you can see anew after the storm. And the storm can be a physical storm, an emotional storm, a mental storm, or even a spiritual storm. A spiritual awakening can occur after a storm. Sometimes a storm is necessary, a turbulence in one's life to make one look afresh. And maybe become aware of spiritual essences and presence, of your own spiritual presence and essence.

Sometimes there is darkness before the storm, and after the storm there is a lightness, a new horizon, and a new awareness. So, one can view a storm as a clearing of the way, like an old broom sweeping up the old dirt, clearing the path of debris, allowing for a clear pathway forward.

If life was always smooth, you would not learn, and we have said this before.

Rains are necessary in a desert in order for the desert to flower. The blooms in a desert may just be brief, but they serve a purpose. Some deserts were once covered by water and now are arid. Some areas were under water and are now visible and seen, creating new life in the oceans, in the world. So, there is always change; things happening. Destruction in some places and creation in others. And sometimes destruction has to happen for creation to occur. Do not fear this.

Resisting change can cause its own problems. Be prepared to 'go with the flow'. Like the tree that bends with the wind, if the tree is too brittle and does not bend, it can break. Habits become comfortable, routine, and secure, and you need some of that.

Be open to change when it occurs. Try not to resist because opportunities can occur with change. Presents that you were not expecting; opportunities can occur. Try not to get stuck in a rut. Question what you are doing with your life. Are you where you wish to be; are you achieving what you wish to achieve? Do not change for change's sake. Let your feelings be your guide. If you are content and at ease, then why change? But if you question where you are, why you are, what you are achieving, and why you are here, then maybe it is time. Because you are being stirred mentally to question what you are doing with your life.

And you can seek outside yourself for the answer, but you will receive *so* much more wisdom if you go within; to listen to that still small voice, that guidance within you. Yes, you get busy with life, but try to give some time each day to communicating within, communicating with your own spirit, your own essence.

Ask questions and be open to the way in which you receive a reply. Replies come in many ways; through inspiration, dreams, 'knowing', and conversations with friends and family.

Give yourself the gift of time to spend alone for a few minutes each day, so that you can enrich your life and enrich yourselves 'knowing' that you are spirit in a human body. And acknowledge the essence that you truly are; a universal energetic being experiencing life at this present time.

You are surrounded by seen and unseen energies. We are here to support you, love you and encourage you on your individual paths.

Celebrate the gift of life and nurture it well. Take care of yourselves and take care of others. Service to mankind is one of the highest attributes you can have. Look around and see how you can be of service to your family, friends, your neighbours, your community, your country, and the world.

And start with the first step. Keep it simple and know that *you* can make a difference day by day.

Enjoy the honour of having been given a life to experience.

We love you; we cherish you, we harmonise with you, and we encourage you to harmonise with us… your unseen support.

Namaste, Shalom, Salaam, Auf Wiedersehen.

Talk 25 – With Elaine and Georgie

7th December 2020

Enjoy the laughter, enjoy the bright side of things in life. Laughter is healing, enjoyment, being in joy. Laughter lifts the spirit. Try whenever possible to see the humour in life. Not that you need to be silly but allow yourselves to lighten your loads with humour.

Humour at no one's expense; inclusive not exclusive. Laughter is like the tinkling of bells, a high vibration, a healing vibration. Be in the joy of the moment. Laugh at the silly things of life. Laughter is like an internal massage of the organs. Laughter is healing.

We encourage you to be full of joy and laughter, but at nobody's expense. Laugh with each other, and see the funny side of life, for there is much that can make you sad, especially during difficult times. So, take the time to find the humour of life, the funny, endearing moments.

Try not to take yourselves too seriously. Remember that life is like a short play, a short experience in your eternal life. There will be serious events, and there will be some sadness, but on the whole, we encourage you to be on the bright side, to see the silliness of things.

You can learn with laughter. Sometimes the lesson is absorbed more easily with laughter and remembered well afterwards. Respect others' senses of humour; respect their values.

Try not to cause offence. Do not make cartoons of Mohammed when that religion wishes no imagery, only words. Respect the values of others. Try not to cause upset unnecessarily. Do not 'tease the bear'. When one causes damage or insult to another, there is nothing amusing or funny about that; so respecting others' values is important.

Respect the way each religion worships, for each one has a grain of the truth. Each one is trying to connect with their godliness, with their God, in whatever form it comes.

Like many mountain paths going up the mountain, each religion has its own path, but its ultimate aim is to reach the top of the mountain. So, respect their journeys. Try not to focus on the extremists of any religion, for there will always be some who will be extreme or radical in their interpretation of their religion. But look to the majority. Study the religions so that you know the truth, so that you get to see the pearls of each religion. For each religion has something to offer, some wisdom, some pointer towards God.

Do not believe that yours is the only way, for there are many paths up the mountain. Let people be free to choose which path they wish to take. Do not be judgemental. Be accepting of others unless they are causing harm. In which case pray for them, and ask for healing for their disturbed minds, their distorted views.

For it is love that will erase the dis-ease and the dislike of others; the jealousies that so often are petty. The beliefs of hate and the need to incite hatred is so unnecessary, harmful, and evil.

Seek to love, seek to embrace others, and seek to harmonise with others and their viewpoints whenever possible. Bring lightness into your experience of life whenever possible; the lightness of laughter, the lightness of not taking yourself too seriously.

This is merely a speck of time in your experience. No one is so important that they cannot laugh at themselves. Harmonise with your humour, but do not be vulgar with it or cruel. Laugh with lightness. Laughter stimulates the immune system to help healing. So, in the middle of disease, seek for the moments of lightness, of humour. Try to lessen worries whenever possible. Try to lessen stress whenever possible. Surround yourself with love and lightness of being.

Always remember to let others know that you care for them, that you love them. Do not be fearful of stating this fact if it is true for you.

There is never enough love expressed in this world. And the more that love is expressed, and peace is nurtured, the less war there will be, fewer battles, and less stress.

Life is to be enjoyed whenever possible. If you are not living in joy, ask yourself why? Ask yourself what you need to do to be able to enjoy the majority of your days, whether working or playing.

If you are feeling stressed in life, this is not good. This is not good for the soul and the spirit. This leads to disease, to mental distress and down-heartedness. Seek occupations that bring you joy and where you can help others.

Seek to help nature and nurture yourselves in the process. Be of good cheer whenever possible. Harmonise with your life, create harmony in your life. Ensure that you have time for laughter; that you are never too busy to laugh and have humour. Be filled with laughter and mirth. Be prepared to laugh at yourselves from time to time. You need to take your responsibilities seriously, but you can still enjoy yourself whilst doing so.

Be in an occupation that brings you joy in your life, in your heart. That enriches you, enriches your spirit and your soul, as well as your bank balance!

You see, we recognise some realities of life, so be responsible; be able to respond. And if you are in the wrong job or occupation; if you are in such a situation that you are not in enjoyment; be prepared to change responsibly.

If you are in disharmony within yourself, reach out for help. Do not suffer alone. Do not allow the clouds of being in disharmony to overwhelm you. Reach out for help and support, for it will not always be dark and stormy. Storms pass: situations usually improve over time. So, if you feel overwhelmed, reach out to us in Spirit, and reach out to others who can help you ease your path, ease your disturbance.

Allow yourselves from time to time to not be strong. Allow that you are human and can be vulnerable. When you feel weak, ask for help from others. You do not have to go through this journey of life alone.

Remember to come within, to hear the still small voice of your inner wisdom, your knowing. And to hear the still small voice of God and of your spirit helpers, your support. For we are always here with you. And we too, in Spirit, have humour and laughter, enjoyment and lightness of spirit.

Each moment in your life is precious; your life is valuable. Enjoy it to the full.

Make changes if you need to, for the betterment of your soul. Remember to do no harm to others. Take care of yourselves and be full of light and joy, moment to moment.

Be in peace. Celebrate living whenever possible.

We love you. You are precious to us, very precious.

Be full of light and laughter.

Auf Wiedersehen, Namaste, Shalom, Salaam.

Talk 26 – With Elaine and Georgie

14th December 2020

Dear children, we are the Council of Twelve and we welcome you today. We are happy to be here in your presence. We bring you healing, and we bring our love and our caring.

Be open to the Universe and the miracles that take place, seen and unseen. For there are wonders all around you. But sometimes you are blind to seeing these. So, keep your eyes open for the miracles that take place. Very often they are small but significant. Do not dismiss them as imagination; try not to doubt what you see. Try to see with believing eyes, with openness like a child. Have the innocence of the child within you and let wonderment fill your soul. Miracles take place on a daily basis if you have the eyes to see. Little precious moments that can so easily be dismissed and discarded. Embrace them, observe them, be open to them, for they will enrich your soul. So have your feet firmly planted on this Earth, yet allow your spirit, yourself, to be open to the miracles of every day.

(Pause... Shift of energy? Slightly deeper voice.)

We give you our greetings and our love. We enjoy coming to see you and being with you, and we thank you for this opportunity, this space that you give us.

Timing is everything. Time on your planet is necessary for organization, for practicality. We in heaven do not need time such as you know it. For what appears to you to be many hours can be like a speck of time in ours, a fleeting moment of time. So, time is a perception, yet for you to function on earth, time is required. Morning, Noon, Nighttime, days and weeks, months and years. Depending where you are on earth, times will be different. For noon where you are is not noon on the other side of the earth.

So, there is day and night. When there was no interconnectedness, one part of the world did not know that the other part of the world was different. But now there is an awareness and an ability to cope with the differences between day and night. The time zones, as you call them. So somewhere on Earth the Sun is shining. It may not be on your part of the Earth at a given time. So, when it seems dark to you, be aware that it is light elsewhere, and your turn will come. The arising of the Sun will occur in time. And the setting of the Sun is necessary for you to get rest, relax, sleep, and to heal. All is in balance.

And sometimes you have a problem, an issue that seems overwhelming, that seems so difficult. When you have done all, you can to fix the problem, then trust, let go of the issue and let God and us assist. Often you hold so tightly that you do not let go and trust God. Letting go and trusting God can be so hard. The words seem simple, but the reality is difficult. Trust in the order of things. Trust that you have eternity to get it right. Trust that timing is everything. It may not be time for an event to occur. So, trust that there will come a time when it is right for the event to happen. You cannot rush time. Everything has its place, its order. There is an order in life as there is in nature. Sometimes the ordering of life is hard to comprehend, hard to understand, such as this pandemic. You wonder why? Why are people suffering and dying? Maybe there is an order even though it is not easily seen. We have said before that there are no accidents. Sometimes you cannot see the bigger picture.

So, try to trust the process. And maybe all will be revealed at a later date. Certainly, you have seen the clearing up of your atmosphere and less pollution during this time.

We hope this event will help you value each other more. To appreciate what you have in life. To take care of yourselves and of others. To cease being selfish. To see the bigger picture and how you have an effect in this world.

That disharmony, battles, and wars hurt so many unnecessarily.

How important it is to lay down weapons of war and struggles of power.

How important it is to learn the value of life. If you valued life, you would not allow wars to happen because people die. No-one wins.

Embrace your brethren, your fellow travellers. Love each other.

Treasure each other and their right to live. Tolerate your differences. Learn to live together in peace and harmony, or else you will end up destroying your world. For what and why?

Extend the hand of friendship, of peace. Learn to love. This is not always easy. Honour the spirit and the soul that is in each one of you. Be gentle with yourselves, be kind to each other. Be kind to yourselves.

Harmony begins with you. If you are in a state of peace and harmony, it is difficult to extend the hand of war, the fist, the hate.

Be in peace whenever possible. Love one another as we love you. Be gentle and kind with each other, starting with yourselves.

Trust that you can make a difference each and every day and look for the miracles of life.

Remember that life is like a kindergarten where you play and learn.

All of you are children. Children of God and the Universe. Learn to play nicely. Do this now; do not wait.

Timing is everything. Act now and make a difference in your world.

Amen, Auf Wiedersehen, Namaste, Shalom, Salaam.

God Bless You All.

Talk 27 – With Elaine and Georgie

21st December 2020

All is well, as well as can be expected under the circumstances. Cease your worry and your anxiety. Relax and let go. Trust that everything is perfect in its timing. So, you can indeed let go of the reins and 'allow.' Just be in the present, in the now, and all is well.

(Referring to Georgie's Father-in-Law, who is transitioning currently? Long one-minute pause.)

Let it go. Let the worries that worry you… let them go. Try to be in a state of peace whenever possible. Trust that all is as it should be, for there is a pattern, which sometimes you cannot see. You have to trust, moment by moment. Be the best that you can be. Not perfect, but just be the best you can be; just 'BE'. Sometimes just take a moment to breathe, to sit, to be aware. Take a pause in the busyness of life. Look at the skies, look at nature; take a deep breath and cease the rushing, just for a few moments.

We have so much love for you, and we want you to have love for yourselves. Love yourselves, fill yourself with love, the Love of Spirit, the love of God. Turn off the noise, the negativity and just be in the now, in the Presence. And enjoy the richness, the quality of the moment. You may not know what is about to happen, and sometimes you are not supposed to know. It just is, moment by moment, step-by-step.

There is a saying that the journey starts with the first step. But you cannot see the journey's end because you are where you are, at the first step.

So, when you focus on love and loving yourself and being kind to others, your steps will always be right. Sometimes you might stumble, but you will correct yourself.

It is like a large, large stone that you cannot see around. So, you have to walk around it to see what is beyond it. That is where the journey occurs, the walking towards it, around it, so that you can see beyond. So, sometimes the path is not clear; it is obscured like the big, big rock that could be in your way of vision, your line of seeing. So, try not to look too far ahead because all you really have is now, this moment, this breath.

You may be here tomorrow, and you may not. So, do not be in fear; just be in the moment. You do not always have to know all the answers. As you walk the path you will learn the answers. As you walk around the boulder, so you see what is behind it.

Each step has value and has richness. So, do not be in such a hurry to get to the end of the journey that you miss the richness of each step, the viewpoint from each step. For if you are so busy trying to reach the sea you may miss the mountain, the valley, the scenery before the sea. So, you reach the sea and you have not seen what you have passed or gone through, so you are poorer for that.

Embrace the journey, embrace the travelling, embrace each step. Take notes along the way. It may be a person that you pass; by a smile or a word that enriches your journey. Or it may be a bird on a branch of a tree; that you may miss its song if you are rushing by.

Enjoy moment to moment. And then your journey's end will be even richer, of more value to you; you will have learnt more.

Try to keep things simple and not overcomplicate things. Enjoy the beauty of the moment, for if you look for the beauty, you will see it. Open your eyes and see all there is to see. The well can be deep, or it can be shallow. Plunge its depths, explore; enrich yourselves by the experience.

Do not rush through life. You are not here for long anyway, so savour each moment.

Lessons can be learnt even in difficult times. Unexpected lessons. For when you view something in one direction, if you see it from another direction you see something different.

Be prepared to consider your options and your viewpoints. Likewise, respect others' viewpoints, beliefs, and religions. Do not mock them, for what is right for you may not be right for someone else. Do not enforce your beliefs on others. Allow them their own learnings, their own teachings. Respect another's point of view. Respect their journey, for they walk a different path from you. Neither is better. It just is. Judge not another, for you have no idea what they have gone through, their trials and tribulations. You can always learn from others. And you have the freedom of choice. You do not have to believe in what they believe, but you may. Do not be stubborn with your viewpoint. Allow others to have their views. And do not let others negate your viewpoint.

Enjoy your journey whenever possible and remember that it is during difficult times that you learn the most. So, try to see the jewel in every moment. Sometimes it is hard to see. And sometimes, you can only see with hindsight.

Value your life, for you have been given a gift. Treasure your gift. Nurture yourself. And love yourself, for you are a child of God. You are Spirit incarnate. And you have so much to offer.

Find your gift within you; nurture it, develop it; for it is God given. Do not waste your gift. Part of the joy of life is to find what your gift is. Do something that makes your heart sing.

Resonate with happiness. Let your journey through life resonate with happiness, for life is also a gift.

Enjoy each moment that you are given, while you are here.

Give thanks and look for the bounty, not the famine. Focus on the many gifts you have.

And be grateful, for you are alive; you are exploring; you are developing and learning.

Enjoy your journey, moment to moment, step-by-step.

We walk with you, we love you, and we give you our blessings. Amen, Auf Wiedersehen, Shalom, Salaam.

Talk 28 – With Georgie and Elaine

13th January 2021

I ASKED: 'WHAT OR WHO IS GOD?'

Children, you are welcome, most welcome to join with us, and we likewise are pleased to join with you. We are the Council of Twelve and we are here nearby you, with you. Allow fears to be scattered. Feel us nearby, for we are right next to you, blending with you, with all three of you. And it is I, Abdullah, also here to greet you (me "and Maria Magdalena de Pazzi, I feel her essence with us").

Dear ones, you ask questions about God. What is God? Who is God? GOD IS. God is eternal. The Essence of God is Good, Pure Love, Magnificence. There is a pure energy that exists. An All Knowing and All Being. There is no end to God, for God is the Universe; is the Energy, the Heartbeat of the World and of the Worlds. God is Infinite, Immeasurable, Magnanimous, All Loving Energy. And we are mere servants of that. We aim towards that; to that purity of essence, of doing good, peace and harmony.

We are at one level; you are at another, and we are all aiming to progress towards that Light; that Infinite Spark, the Duality of Being. So, we revere God, the Essence. We have to give IT a name, and different people give IT different names, that Essence of Goodness, of Wholeness, that Spark.

You are able to get nearer and nearer to God as you evolve.

As we progress, we become closer; as you progress you become closer. That closeness comes with wisdom, experience, and knowledge. We are a group of Spirits that work at one level, and you are a group of Spirits that work at a different level: Spirit on Earth.

The Essence of God is Pure Love. As we said before, The Heartbeat of the World. The All-Knowing.

Some of you call him God; some of you call him Allah. There are many names but just one God.

Our aim is to become closer to that One Essence. To become more illumined with the knowledge, the Brightness of God. When you add a zero or an O to God, it becomes Good. Goodness and mercy; blessing the Infinite. You cannot quantify God with a body; it is an Energy, an Essence. Some humans like images; others choose to have no image, just the word that signifies God. The American Indians worshipped nature and their all-knowing God, Spirit. Hindus, Buddhism and all the religions of the world worship this One Essence that has many names.

The purer you are, the kinder you are, the closer you become like God. And there is a particle of God within each and every one of you. That is a drop of the essence of the energy of God within each and every one. No one is better than another. One may have more wisdom, more insight, more knowing, more conscious awareness of Spirit and God, but does that make them wiser or smarter or less like God than another?

Each of you are blessings; each of you are children of this energy, this Universal Source of Love. Like rain has raindrops, each of you has a drop of this essence within. Your job on Earth is to remember this. Remember the essence of who you truly are. Remember your Godlikeness. The good part of you. There is infinite wisdom, infinite love, and infinite divine love that can never run out. So, allow yourselves to be surrounded by this love, for you are a part of it. Sometimes you choose to turn away from it and that is your choice, your freedom to do so. This does not make you wrong; this is simply a choice that you have.

This love is *always* there for you, always with you. But sometimes you choose to shut your eyes and look away. When you are ready, we encourage you to turn back; open your eyes and look for that love, the love that is within you. The still small voice we have talked about; the essence of who you truly are. Not your clothes, not your money, not your material goods, but you, your naked soul, your spirit that resides within your body.

Your body is the vehicle which carries this essence. Take care of this body, for without this body you cannot be on Earth. So, it is your duty to nurture your body, take care of it and look after it for as long as you need it. And when you no longer need it, you can cast it off like an overcoat, like an envelope. And you emerge from that and come back to the World of Spirit, without a body.

And here in Spirit you continue to learn, explore, progress and evolve. Progressing along the path to be closer to the God Source, to the Essence of Love; to the Chalice of Love, of Golden Light.

Allow your cup, your chalice to overflow whenever possible. Fill your chalice with love. Fill your soul, your essence, with the love of God. This does not mean you need to be on bended knee in a church, synagogue, a religious place. For God is everywhere. God is around the corner, in the garden, in nature, in your neighbour and your friend. See the God within them. See the God essence within your friends and neighbours, for each of you has it. Just sometimes you choose to shade it away and not let that essence shine forth.

Consciously connect with this God Source whenever possible, while still carrying on your normal life. Do not be so absorbed with it that you forget to live your life, because that is why you are on Earth, to live a human life. Spend part of your day communicating with your God source within yourself, your inner self.

Do not judge your body as being inadequate, for it is your necessary vehicle to be on Earth. Nurture your body and nurture your inner self. Remember, you are *always* a child of God and aim to do good.

Be kind to yourselves and be kind to others. Fill your own chalice with kindness and love and allow it to out-pour to others. Fill your own cup before you try to give to others because when your cup overflows, you give naturally with no strain, no stress. Do no harm to yourself or others. Live your life based in love. Love of friend, love of neighbour, love for yourself and love of God. God is always there.

Choose when you are ready to turn towards the God light, the good light of gentleness, kindness, peace, and harmony. Remember when you become fractious that often this is because you feel uncomfortable within. So, sit for a while to become comfortable within, and then you will feel less fractious, less stressed, less disturbed. Your essence will be more harmonious. Spread this harmony around yourself and those you love and equally those you do not love. Mentally give them your blessings and allow them to walk their path. Remember the goodness within you. No one is bad. Every one of you has a drop of this Essence within, just that some of you forget and turn away from this God essence.

Let there be no dogma, no strict rules, no penitence; for God does not need this; God is so much more. God is Pure Light. And you are part of that pure light. So, walk in that Light, remembering that Light. Do not judge yourselves so harshly. Try not to judge yourselves at all. Be aware, be gentle with yourselves. Strive to learn, to grow, to do no harm and to love others. And love yourself, for there is only one of you; you are unique. You are a child of God and are beautiful. Walk in peace and harmony. Turn your face towards the God Light and struggle less. Play with the Light; be light-filled and enjoy your life, your God given life. Respect your life, be grateful for it and learn with it.

Enjoy your gift of life and love yourself, for you are indeed worthy of that. Never let anyone tell you less. You are a gift from God. You are God's gift to Earth. You are God manifested on Earth. Remember your goodness, your beloved essence.

You are enough because you are a child of God. Love yourself and love God, for you are connected forever. Live in peace, harmony, and love.

Amen Shalom, Salaam, Namaste, Auf Wiedersehen. Blessings to you all, dear children.

Talk 29 – With Elaine and Georgie

19th January 2021

CHANGE

Dear ones, we are gathering again today with you; Council of Twelve and Abdullah and Maria Magdalena de Pazzi. We come as a team to fill you with hope and balance. The balance of being grounded in the Earth, with your head in the universe, being the blend of body and spirit that you are.

We know that you like permanence and solidity, and yet life is full of impermanence, change, the ebb, and flow of life. There is no such thing as permanence. There may be permanence of a building, a street, because this is hard material. But when you look at nature, there is always impermanence, always movement. Seasons change, and with the seasons changing, nature changes. And there is repetition, so in a way there is permanence. But each time a season comes around, it is slightly different. It is not the same form. Like you yourselves change bodies periodically through cells dying and cells being reborn. You are not the same body that you were ten years ago, fifty years ago. Yes, you were smaller then and bigger now. But yet your bone is not the same as the bone you had when you were younger, the blood is not the same, the tissues have also changed and grown, so there is impermanence.

However, the permanent thing is your soul, your spirit, the core of you. It changes, it grows and develops, but the essence of you is the same. Maybe earlier you were more naive, and now you are wiser.

Allow change to happen; do not resist it. For change is natural; change is normal. And when you are in fear, you fear change. And there is much change occurring now on planet Earth. Not only change of illness and disease and death more frequently occurring or becoming more obvious. But there is a change in the atmosphere; it is cleaner. Rivers and seas are slightly cleaner because less pollution is occurring at present. And systems of living are being reviewed and reassessed by all of you. It is like a big question time at the moment; What is happening? What will happen? What has happened? But you will see progress and change, and we believe you will see the betterment of society. More respect for nature and for each other.

There has always been change throughout the aeons. If that were not so, you would still be on all fours, so change always occurs. So, change is progress, change is evolution; nothing is permanent. Even the solid buildings break down over time. What was a modern building becomes an ancient one given time. What was modern becomes old; what is solid can become liquid given an earthquake.

Seasons change, the tides move, and you grow. Try to trust that within all the change, there is meaning. And then there is the certainty that you *are* spirit, you *are* soul, *you are a part of God*.

Realise that you are all, each nation, going through change. Each day changes, for you may wake up one day and the sun is shining, and you may wake up the next and it is raining. No two days are the same all the way through the day. And you change, not only in how you grow but also your beliefs, your hobbies, your occupations and they are all learnings.

The more you can be grounded and connected with your

spirit, the less you will worry about these changes. You will accept them with more grace. You will trust them, and you will be excited about them because they will beckon new horizons for you, new events. Change stops you from being stale, stops you from not growing. Because if things were always the same, you would never learn new lessons.

So, explore your Earth when you can. Be aware of the wonders in your Earth, on your Earth. Be aware of civilisations that have gone before, who may have known of many things that you now no longer know about. So, treasure your history and your backgrounds, yet be prepared to move forward with an exploring and inquisitive spirit.

Ask us, "Show us more, tell us more. How can we walk on the correct path?" We are happy to guide you, lead you and show you the way, but we can only do this if you ask for us to assist.

When you check in with us you can become more reassured in your adventure. You can become more reassured that you are on the right path for you, as doors will keep on opening, and you will find there will be no barriers. The obstacles will not be there because it is the path you are supposed to be on. The path will be easy and smooth, and everything will feel right to you.

If you like you can call it an illumination (enlightenment); you illuminate your knowing by checking in with us. Checking in daily when you can just so that you reconnect with the spiritual aspect of yourselves. So, when in doubt, turn to us for reassurance, illumination, and guidance, and you will find that your path is smoother. Not without complications from time to time because it is these complications that increase your learning and your wisdom. But generally, your path will be easier. And when things occur that seem so wrong, that make you question, "where there is a God or is there a God?" We again encourage you to turn towards us, to connect with Spirit for reassurance, for illumination.

Illuminate your life with the wisdom of Spirit. A modern phrase 'touch base with us' on a regular basis so we can reassure and guide. However, it is always your initiative, your choice where you go, and how you go about your life. And if you have done wrong, ask for forgiveness and then move on. For you will make mistakes from time to time. The key is to recognise the mistake, check if you have hurt anyone or harmed anything and ask for forgiveness if you have. Forgiveness both of the person you have harmed as well as from God; try to live your life in harmony. Be willing to be the peacemaker and extend the hand of friendship. Extend the hand of friendship first, for we all wish to be loved, and we all wish to help others. But sometimes there can be defensiveness which prevents us from doing that.

Try to recall your childlike innocence and openness and bring that energy into your present day. Keep life simple, for life is simple but can be made overcomplicated. The simplicity of children can be copied into your adult life. Keep it simple. Be loving, be kind to yourselves and to others, and do no harm.

Live your life *in* peace. Put down weapons of war; do not take up weapons of war, and if no one takes up the weapons there can be no wars. Question your actions, and if they will cause harm, then do not do them.

Remember, there will be an accounting of what you have done in your life. Not to be penalised and punished but an accounting, a record of what you have done. You chose to come here to learn and not to do harm. So, when you come home to us, it will be good to be able to say, "I have learnt, and I have done no harm to myself or others."

Keep it simple, learn well, and live well.

Aim to be happy. And to be thankful for the opportunity you have to be here on Earth, experiencing a life.

Go in peace, live in peace, BE at peace with yourselves and your neighbours.

Amen. Salaam, Shalom, Auf Wiedersehen. Our blessings dear children.

Talk 30 – With Georgie

3rd February 2021

'Ahlan wa Sahlan.' Greetings. This is Abdullah and the Council of Twelve. We are greeting you this day. We are honoured to come into your presence, and we thank you for giving time for us to speak with you.

Wisdom, being wise. Sensing where you need to be, where you need to go. Being open to the opportunities that are around you. Being sensitive to these opportunities and being willing to move towards them. The world is like a stage. You come to the world to perform, to function, to enact your life's meaning, your life's lesson. Once learnt, you return to Spirit, and in Spirit you continue to learn. There are many houses of learning, research, libraries that you can choose to explore and become even yet wiser. Long corridors with doors opening to different rooms of learning. Different establishments; learning establishments, arts, music. Green spaces where you can sit and breathe the pure air.

You can learn just by encountering a human being. You don't always need books and computers. Sometimes your learning is a simple exchange of talking. Listen for those droplets of knowledge; follow your 'aha' feeling. If something resonates with you, follow it, explore it, and research it. When you have learnt enough then look for your next 'aha' moment. If you check in with us frequently, we can also help you and guide you. But we cannot lead your life for you. That is for you to do, that is your role in the play of life. It must be you that experiences, you that enjoys, you that hurts, you that puts together the tapestry of your life, stitch by stitch, moment by moment.

Be aware, and open to listening to words said by friends. Sometimes at nighttime, go over these conversations so you can recall what was said. See if there are any pearls of wisdom within those conversations that you may have missed in the moment. There is much to learn and many ways to learn. A walk in nature, in the forest, by the sea is a learning experience. Studying in a library is yet another. Even having an argument with a friend or relation is a learning experience. Nothing is wasted if you choose to observe. And the reason you are here on this planet is you can learn more deeply by having experiences, person-to-person experiences. The rough with the smooth helps to deepen your learning and your wisdom. Life is smoother when you are in Spirit.

So, this Earth is rather like a school of learning. Not just when you are in the classroom as a child, but each day. You can learn until you die. And be thankful for the learning experiences that you have. You will meet up with the loved ones that have gone ahead of you. You will have time to play with them and learn with them and be with them, and they will greet you with great joy. But until then, learn to live fully as a human being on the planet Earth. Explore all that you can; do not waste this opportunity of life.

Be kind to yourself and to one another. Try not to overeat, over drink, over smoke, over anything. Keep your life in balance. Try not to numb out with drugs, busyness, and the adrenaline rush. Remember to tell those that you love that you love them. Do not wait for them to be dying before you tell them. And allow yourself to experience their love in return, the love of a friend, child, lover, or animals. Keep open.

Each of you is like a blade of grass; sometimes you get crumpled on, sometimes you grow, but there is always growth. Imagine you are a blade of grass with the Sun shining on you, keeping you warm, keeping you healthy. Raise your face to the Sun; even when it is behind the clouds. When you feel down, look up. Remember consciously your connection with God, the universe, and fellow spirits.

Remember to remember that you are spirit in human form. Acknowledge your spiritual part; touch base with us. Fill your void with self-nurturing, kindness, and gentleness.

The oceans are many and yet all are the same substance of water. You are made of water to a large part. When you mass together as groups, you are like oceans; yet each one of you is an individual. Allow your individuality to shine forth and be prepared to ebb and flow. Sometimes you will be quiet; sometimes you may be stormy; sometimes you will be in full flow like a full tide. Other times you will be quiet and reflective with just a gentle ripple.

Each one of you has different characteristics and different qualities. Don't try to be like others. Be proud of your uniqueness, your individuality. Each of you is unique, so allow your uniqueness to shine. Do not be afraid to stand out. Because by showing your light, your uniqueness, you can give strength to others to show their true light; instead of trying to hide in the crowd.

Always remember that you have the right to be here, and no one has the right to crush your light; to hide your uniqueness. Be proud, stand tall. You can be humble while doing this; you do not need to be brash or full of ego. Stand in your own true path, do not betray yourself. Honour yourself. So that when you return to us, you have nothing to be ashamed of. Because you have been given a gift of uniqueness; no two of you are alike. You may be similar but not alike.

So, let the gem that you are shine forth, like a jewel. Treasure yourself. And if you have a gift, other than just being yourself, be and help others show theirs. Shine by example.

Trust is a small word but a big action. Trust that you will know when you are on the right path for you, not someone else, for you. On your unique path, your unique journey, your unique act, as in a play. You can be unique as well as blend with others. So being unique does not mean being lonely. You will find others that resonate with you. And by your shining forth, you make others brave; you give them strength, you give them an example. Be proud of who you are, not arrogant, proud. For you have many blessings and many gifts. Seek them out, be grateful for them, and acknowledge them. These are gifts you have been given for your play, for your journey, and your life on the planet.

Allow yourself to sparkle. Walk with lightness in your heart and lightness in your feet whenever possible. And give thanks for your gift of life; never take it for granted. Enjoy each and every moment whenever possible. Remember that it is a learning experience and a play. And with each day you gain more wisdom and more experience.

Trust your feelings; the inner voice inside you. If something doesn't feel right, then it probably is not right for you. It may be right for your neighbour, but not for you. That doesn't make your neighbour or you wrong; it simply is.

Even as part of a team you can still shine your light. Be grateful for each day; never assume you will be here tomorrow. So, enjoy each day to the full, so that when you come back to us, you can say to yourself, "I have led a full life. I have learnt a lot.

I have achieved what I set out to do, and I am ready to come home." Try not to be, "I wish I had; I should have done." Grab every opportunity you have, hold it with both hands and explore it. And when it has ceased to teach you, then move on to your next lesson. You are only here for a short amount of time. Even if you live to be 100, it will still seem like a short amount of time. So, live fully, gratefully; learning, exploring, playing.

Enjoy life as you are living it. Do not wait until you become too old to enjoy.

Learn, love, laugh, explore. Be happy.

Namaste, Shalom, Salaam, Auf Wiedersehen. Go with our blessings dear ones. Amen.

Talk 31 – With Elaine and Georgie

11th February 2021

'Ahlan wa Sahlan.' It is I, Abdullah, here with you today. Others may join, but presently it is just I. Greetings, my Children.

Astronomy was my love and still is. The Universe is magnificent. Full of so many Planetary Objects, so many stars, the Milky Way, Orion's Belt, and different constellations. And each day they turn a little so that at one point in time, Orion's Belt will be in one place, and at another point in time, it is elsewhere. It is still the same Constellation, the same space between each star that makes up the Constellation; yet it, as a whole, has moved.

So, you see, there is always movement; nothing is ever still. Even things that appear to be the same can shift; can be seen in a different light. The stars twinkle and shine, and that is what you are, like stars twinkling and shining, each in your own orbit, your own life path. Yet you also are alongside other stars. So, although you are unique and special, so is everyone else. Each star has its rightful place in the Universe, as do you. There is no such thing as Chaos. Everything is planned and set. There may appear to be Chaos, but very often, that Chaos is within the Plan.

There is a Universal Law, a Universal Plan, and you are a part of that Plan. So, you are needed here on Earth, at present. Because without you, Earth would not be the same. You create an Energy that is Unique and needed. Without you, it would be like a missing stitch in a tapestry. There would be a hole that would be seen and felt. Never feel that you do not matter. Never ask yourself, "What is the point?" You may not be able to see the point in this very moment but be patient. The point will be revealed in time. Sometimes you are not supposed to see the point because if you did see the point, you would miss out on the opportunities that lead to the point. You would be in such a hurry to get to the point that you would miss out on other learning opportunities. Like the journey to a city, if you are so busy trying to get to the city and rushing there, you miss the richness of the journey, the experiences along the path, along the journey. Do not rush your lives away. Each day is blessed; each day has value for those of you who feel there is no point in you being here. "What's the point? I'm just a waste of space." Never believe this. You are never a waste of space. You are a part of Space, of the Universe. A much-needed stitch within the Universe. Without that Stitch, things could unravel. So do not be in a rush to leave the Planet until it is Your Time. Trust that there is a point. Maybe you can't see it right now, but trust.

When you feel on shaky ground, when you feel uncertain and wobbly, turn within. Turn within to your Central Being, your Innermost Being and your Spirit, and connect with Us to get reassurance. Sometimes that feels like such an effort, and yet it is of high value because it will strengthen your wobbly legs. It will give you reassurance. So, when times seem dark, make the extra effort to connect with Us. Do not rush through your life or cut off your life early because that would be such a waste of one opportunity that you have been given. And it also creates such sadness for your family, friends and loved ones. They need you here and want you here. You have value; you are needed.

Sometimes allow Spirit to carry you, to nurture you when

you are not strong enough to nurture yourself. Be gentle and kind with yourself. Try not to be despondent. Take yourself for walks into Nature and nurture your Soul, your Spirit.

You are part of the Globe of Life. You have been created as a Human Being, and you have grown and learnt. Yet there is so much more to learn and explore. Keep the connection with Universe, with Spirit. Do not get lost in the mundane bits of living on Earth, the shopping, the cleaning. These are just parts of being a Human Being doing activities. They take up just a short part of your life. There is so much more that you can be doing to enrich your Soul, your Mind. Read, study, and learn. Learn to have a full experience of life. Treasure each day. Each day is like a building block, one upon the other. These building blocks become like a wall, a building that contains such wisdom.

Try to surround yourself with Love. Not just from other humans but have yourself in a serene environment whenever possible. Cease from violence, cease from violent games, and violent television.

Look for the loving, nurturing, educational games, videos, and TV. There is so much to learn that is positive. Do not submerge yourself in the negative. It is good to be informed but do not submerge yourself in negative. So, if you could manage 80% of your day in positive energy, see how your life would improve in quality and enrich yourself with that. Make an effort to be positive.

See the many blessings that you have, even when they are hard to see in the moment. Never take things for granted. Appreciate. Be grateful. By being positive and grateful, you will attract more of these energies towards you. Energy follows energy; like energy follows like energy. So, when you are in a state of positivity, you will attract positive-ness. Study the power of the mind, for you truly can create your reality very often.

Again, I remind you to ask Us for help, assistance, and support. We cannot take over; we cannot lead your life for you. But we can aid you, assist you. But you must learn to ask for Us. We cannot just jump in unless there is an emergency where we have to help out. That is when you see Angels appearing, in an emergency situation. Because, if it is not your time to come to Us, we will help you to not come to Us.

When the ground becomes shaky, when you are sad, go for a walk. When you are sad turn your face to the Sun. If the Sun is not there, then imagine the Sun, which is just behind the Clouds. But even the rainbow after the rain is a wonderful blessing. That is part of nature in its true glory. Like the Rainbow of Many Colours, there are many stars. Each of you is a star, as I have said. Remember to shine your star and be part of the Universe, part of a constellation, a gathering of humans. Greet your neighbour, greet a stranger as a friend, just with a smile. There are too many lonely stars out there at present, lonely souls. Remember to smile at those that you meet, even behind your masks. For the energy is seen and felt through your eyes. Remember, when you do this, you are helping another by supporting them with your sparkling eyes.

There is a whole world out there to explore. If you feel bored in your current world, expand it whenever possible. This can be done through many avenues. On your Internet, through your televisions, radios. We are learning how to communicate with you through these vehicles. Like the multi-coloured Rainbow, there are many bandwidths of energy. And if you're feeling a little lower on your bandwidth, just turn the radio dial up so that you can move up to the next bandwidth and feel a little more in tune. In Tune with Us and the Universe.

Never feel you are forgotten. You have many unseen souls supporting you, your friends and family that have gone before. They support you from the Other Side; they watch over you and care for you. Sometimes it may just feel like a rush of wind on your cheek or a touch on your hair. The signs are not obvious but watch for those subtle signs. When you feel something on your leg and nothing is there, it may just be one of your family reaching out to reassure you. Likewise, when the picture tilts on a wall and persists in doing this, it is just one of Us letting you know that we are nearby, usually one of your family or friends.

Remember you are part of the Universe, nothing less, and you are needed to be here. You have worth and value. You are important, to Us, to others and for yourself. Because you are here for a Purpose, do not waste the time you have.

Auf Wiedersehen, Shalom, Salaam.

Go with our Blessings, dear Children. Remember that we love you and always will.

Talk 32 – With Georgie

16th February 2021

We welcome you this day. 'Ahlan wa Sahlan.' Our greetings. There are no accidents, and all is well.

In the rush of life, in the busy day, take time for yourself. Connect with your Source and be of good cheer. Whenever you can, be harmonious to yourself and to others.

Harmony, the word is simple, but the reality is more complex. You have harmony of musical notes that work together. You have the harmony of the equal circles that blend to become the number eight or put on its side, the symbol of eternity. The balance of Yin and Yang; good and evil; black and white. Two opposites attract and balance.

And there is a harmony of you as a person taking care of your physical body and your emotional and your spiritual body. And harmonising with your neighbours, family, and friends.

Think of harmony as a bell that rings, a wise aged bell. Think of how the sound expands outwards from the bell into the atmosphere; and can be heard over many miles. So too your energies impact others; resonate outwards, affecting others. For if you rub someone the wrong way, they then go and, feeling rubbed up the wrong way, they then become irritated with others. So if your bell, your sound, your essence is that of love and harmony, that resonates to the next soul, and to the next soul; you can impact positively others beyond your direct contact, your direct connection.

The universe needs harmony, and there is so much disharmony, discord, distress, and dis-ease. So many of you are needed to ring your clear tones of love and peace; to gradually build up a strong harmony of love. Love of self and love of others.

To love others, you must love yourself first, so fill yourself up with love. Love of your life, love of yourself, gratitude for what you have. Sympathy for others, kindness for others and for yourself. For you are like a fountain, a source. So, you have to make your fountain, your source, harmonious and then spreading that harmony is easy. It takes no effort, it is real, and the sound of the bell is true, not false. Work on yourselves first, make peace with yourself, be kind and loving to yourself.

And those of you that have children, teach them how to love themselves. Let them remember how they were in Spirit. Let them grow strong with self-love and self-worth. Reinforce their beauty to them. Let them stand strong and tall. Teach them how to connect with this, their Source. If they are harmonious, they will be harmonious with their friends; and will have harmony with others. So, nurture your children, for they have been given to you as gifts, as presents, and you have the responsibility of teaching them well. Remember that they, like you, are stars in the universe. Let their joy shine forth. Encourage them to follow their paths. Do not try to change them into something you think they should be. Allow them to discover the reason why they are here.

Sunshine. It spreads light across the world. Likewise, you should spread your 'lightness of being' around the world, starting with yourself, your household and your family and friends. For we have need of much light throughout the world, to increase the harmony, peace and healing in this world.

You have a beautiful soul, each one of you. Honour it. Spend as much time on it as you would spend at the hairdressers or at the make-up counter when you polish your face and your body, and you buy clothes for it. Spend an equal amount of time polishing and nurturing your soul, your spirit, and the sparkle within you. Never let your sparkle be dimmed and diminished.

Imagine harmony being like ripples. Ripples of energy resonating through the atmosphere like ripples in a pond. Your energy can resonate through the atmosphere, ever-expanding; but never draining of you and your essence. Like the fountain you are, just pouring out; ever full and overflowing with love, positive-ness. Every one of you can make a difference.

Trust that whatever you do impacts on the Earth. Be the peacemaker, and that starts with being at peace with yourself. Embrace yourself with love. 'A hug a day keeps the doctor away.' Healthy human touch is so important; it allows you to thrive. So, honour your human connections. And even if you should choose to be alone, you always have Us nearby, beside you, encouraging you on your path.

Elevate your soul with peaceful surroundings and harmony within the home. Bring plants and flowers into your home so that you can bring nature indoors. Ideally, go outdoors to nature. But having nature indoors is also good and beneficial for your essence.

When the sunshine shines, see it, observe it; do not ignore it or dismiss it. Appreciate its warmth, its lightness, its upliftment. Equally appreciate the rain that also nurtures nature. If there is balance between the Sun and the rain, then there is also harmony in nature. Harmonise yourself with nature, nurture nature. Be responsible for the damage that you do on Earth. Make your garden a heaven on earth, your piece of heaven, your piece of harmony.

Try to be content with your lot. Appreciate and take in, inwardly digest, your benefits, the gifts that you have been given. Your warm homes, your clothes, your loved ones. Never take them for granted. Appreciate them and appreciate yourself and the gifts that you have been given. Seek out what resonates in your heart, whether it is arts, music, or nature.

Explore your universe and discover all the wonderful mysteries that are in it. There is so much to discover and learn.

You continue for eternity, and you are here for a short space of time. Fill it well with experiences, with love, with harmony. Bring peace to Earth by being peaceful yourselves.

For when you are peaceful within yourself, you can do no harm.

Remember the symbol of eternity. It continues on, in an ever-moving circuit, balanced on both sides. For you are eternal, and you are meant to be here. You are no accident; your energy is needed.

You *are* important. Become that clear resonance of the bell ringing out. Be the creators of harmony. Replenish your fountain when you need to. You *are* the essence of love.

Namaste. We acknowledge the God within you. Acknowledge the God within others.

Shalom, Salaam, Auf Wiedersehen. Go forward, dear children. We love you. Amen.

Talk 33 – With Elaine and Georgie

24th February 2021

Dear children, we are with you this day, Council of Twelve, Abdullah and Saint Maria Magdalena de Pazzi. We are gathered with you today, and we give you our blessings and our love and gratitude for being here.

A sense of humour is important, for there are many serious parts of your life and these need to be lightened with humour, with laughter. Laughter lifts the energy, lifts the heaviness. So, having laughter with others is healing. Laughter is good medicine, but not at the expense of others. Humour, where all can be included, is healthy. Humour, when it is barbed at someone, is not; it is cruel and should not be done. So never laugh at someone's expense. If anything, laugh at yourself. Try not to take yourself too seriously. Do not become pompous and full of yourself; you have way too many failings to do that.

No one is perfect; you all get it wrong from time to time. That is the part of learning. Like a Christmas tree with bulbs, light bulbs all over. Let them light up the tree; let them sparkle and twinkle. For that brings joy to your hearts; it enlightens you with good feelings. And as the presents are under the tree, look for the presence of Spirit when you laugh. Enjoy letting your spirit laugh; do not take yourself too seriously. At the same time, do not be a fool, for you are not that. You, of course, may choose to play the fool and jest to bring others laughter and enjoyment.

So, balance your seriousness, your learning, your studying, your experiences with lightness and laughter, with joy, happiness, and contentment. Have a 'lightness of being.' Realise you are here for a short time and enjoy this time you have, whenever possible. Laugh with yourself, laugh with friends; be in joy.

Be prepared to look at the humour in life, the funny side. When you make a mistake, laugh at yourself, for you are human.

Enjoy the experience of being, of being you. Do not wish yourself to be someone else. Each of you has a pearl of wisdom. Each of you has learning, and each of you has wisdom. But some wisdom may be in the key of C, and some wisdom may be in the key of G. The wisdom may not be the same, but it is still wisdom. Learn from each other. Do not be so full of yourself that you feel you cannot learn from others.

Yes, you can learn from books; but sometimes the writers of those books, the authors, are not always correct. It is simply their opinion, their viewpoint, and their studying. You may find with your studying another nugget of gold, something they missed. So never assume they know it all. Learn what you can learn from them, but that does not mean that there is not more to learn. So, look at different authors, different writers on the same subject. Because their experience and their learning come from their perspective, from their eyes, and their point of view. And they are human beings, so some of their information may be flawed. Take what you like of what they say, leave what you do not like, and then explore if you choose.

Do your own research, your own learning, to get your viewpoint. When you research and explore, you have a base of your own knowledge with you, your perspective. And there may well be something that the other person missed, some new interpretation.

Interpretation of this current illness (Covid-19) can be different depending on your experience of it. Some see death, dying, and unhappiness; others see improved nature. Both aspects are true. Try to look at the whole subject, not just a small kernel. Like the globe, if you are standing in one country, you cannot see another; yet it is there. Try to look for the whole in everything so that you get the global perspective.

Maximise your experience of life. Be prepared to explore as much as you can. Do not take it for truth what others say to you. Examine the situation with your eyes, your knowing. Likewise, you may find some humour funny and some humour not; it is all in the perspective.

Perspective is individual, and each one of your perspectives is important; it adds to the knowledge base of humanity. So, your opinion counts, your viewpoint counts. Do not allow your viewpoints to be diminished by others. Yet do not be stubborn about your viewpoint; be flexible and open to others. Each ear of wheat is individual yet gathered together it becomes a crop. So individual ideas are important, and together they lead to knowledge. More depth of understanding, more compassion and understanding. Again, we say do not be arrogant, for there are others' viewpoints. But do not be afraid to express your own viewpoint for fear of being laughed at. Because your voice has value, your opinion has value. Do not hide your light behind a bushel. Be prepared to stand tall and express yourself, because your opinion matters.

Likewise, be prepared to hear others, even the voice of children. Often, they have a wisdom, an understanding, a simplicity that grabs at the truth in a more honest fashion; a more easily understood fashion. Where you can get complicated, they can be simple with their wisdom.

Knowledge is powerful, so try to learn something each day, something of value. Do not fritter your time away. See how you can contribute, both to your own knowledge and to the knowledge of others. Keep your ears open so that you can hear the wisdom of others in a simple sentence.

Gold, when it is in the Earth, is a thin line entrapped in a rock of minerals. Yet when gathered together, it becomes an object of value. Likewise, the pieces of information that you gather, as it collects it becomes valuable. Enjoy learning.

Do not waste your time. Become fruitful with your knowledge, and do not be shy in imparting it to others, for they can also learn from you, as you can learn from them. Kernels of truth can be given even in just one sentence. If it resonates with you, there is value.

And as we have said, laughter can be the best medicine. It fills your lungs, it raises your energy, it lightens your spirit. So, give time for humour. Never be so serious that it gets you down. Again, it is about balance. Laughter has a wonderful resonance, the tinkling of bells. Be filled daily with the tinkling of bells, with some laughter. And if you are feeling low, then seek that humour, for it is necessary at that time. It lifts the heaviness of the spirit.

Enjoy your experience; enjoy your life. Learn from the hard parts; laugh at the funny parts. All of life is an experience with which you gather wisdom and learning. Treasure each moment; consider each moment a gift, for that is what it is. You breathe in and your heart beats; you have life. Treasure your life, take care of yourselves and be thankful that you have a life, for it is a gift.

Look at your life with fresh eyes each day. Never take your life for granted. When you wake each day, thank God for your gift, and when you go to bed at night, be grateful. Filled with gratitude for the experiences you have had that day. And then rest well because tomorrow will be full of even more experiences. How lucky you are to be experiencing life in a human body. Be grateful for the experience, for you have been given an opportunity, a blessing, a gift. Use it wisely and use it well. Never let it go to waste. Embrace your day every day because time goes quickly, and you will find there is never enough time, no matter how long you live. So live life to the full and be thankful and remember to laugh and love.

Amen. Peace to you all.

Auf Wiedersehen, Shalom, Salaam.

Talk 34 – With Elaine and Georgie

3rd March 2021

Alleluia means 'Praise God.' And your connection between you and your God is important. God, in truth, is just one; but you humans talk of many gods; you give the same God many names. And if you could just but realise that it is the one God, there doesn't have to be all this in-fighting, all this war against war.

Religious wars are so unnecessary and in vain because you are fighting for the same God's cause.

If you could just remember that you are all the same. All of you have a beating heart, lungs that take in air, loved ones, families, and friends. None of you wants to lose those, and none of you wants to lose your lives in a vain attempt at glory and aspiration.

Cease the battles within, and you will cease the battles without. When you are at war with yourself, it is so easy to turn that dislike outwards and do battle with others. So, to stop wars, you must develop peace within; each one of you. Look at your friends, your neighbours, and strangers around you; you are all the same. Each one of you has an essence of God within you. So, revere your friends, neighbours, and strangers that pass you by, and you pass by. Bless them silently; acknowledge their God given essence. And when you come from an essence of peace, you radiate peace; and others learn by that. We are repeating ourselves, but this is a lesson you need to learn.

Stop taking up arms in the name of God. God does not need it or want it. War is a man-created, not a God-created force. There is no honour, patriotic duty or goodness in war.

It is up to each one of you to say, "Stop, Enough, No."

If you do not take up arms, there can be no armies. Politicians may talk of war, but if there is no one to go to war, then war cannot be created. Politicians have to resort to communication and negotiation; and learn to give way, to balance, so that there is a win/win. So that no one loses face, but you each equally come to a balance and an agreement.

Harmony on your planet must take place. Otherwise, you will indeed destroy yourselves, and for what and why? For a piece of land, for a bit of power, which counts as nothing in the realm of time. Learn to be peace full, filled with peace. So that battles are abnormal, unusual. So that peace and harmony are the normal.

Take care of yourselves; love yourselves and love each other. Take care of your sick, your wounded, your neglected. Empower the weak; help them recognise their God self. Give them hope and encouragement. Help them to believe in themselves so that they can reignite their light within themselves; and not be lost in despair and depression and drugs.

You are each born a soul, full of hope, full of excitement, coming here to the planet to grow and learn. And you can grow and learn by helping your neighbours; by helping ones who do not do so well as yourselves. You earn your 'Brownie points' by doing this. You enlighten your soul by doing this, not by gaining money and wealth and lands, but by strengthening your neighbour and those who are unloved by society. Putting out a helping hand to help raise another; so that you both win. You win by feeling good, and the person that you reach your hand out to wins; by getting more of a blessing and a boost to re-living again rather than sinking downwards into despond. One helping hand can make such a difference. You may think that's not so, but to the one who is down, seeing a hand coming to help them raises them up physically, emotionally, and mentally. And if they receive a helping hand each day, they can become stronger.

So, focus on helping others rather than going to war with each other. You all come to this planet with excitement, to learn, not to die early from unnecessary battle, pride, or propaganda.

Question authority when they tell you to go to war. If you all question it, then how will they manage to get you to go to war? Each one of you stand up; and together you become a crowd, a movement; and you can make a change for the better.

Your responsibility is to make peace, not war. War is embattlement, and there is no need to battle your brethren, your neighbours, your fellow human beings.

Look your 'so-called enemy' in the face and see their God essence and let them see yours. No matter what colour your skins, no matter what nationality you are, have an open hand, not a closed fist. You will find if you are full of love, you cannot close a fist easily against another. It is counterintuitive.

Each one of you has the responsibility to make peace each day. When your anger rises up, train yourself to let it go appropriately. Take a deep breath and think again. By doing this, each one of you can teach each other by example. Some of you do this already, but the majority do not. So, help teach your fellow human being, your neighbour, simply by being the best you can be. Filled with love and generosity, kindness; to yourself and then to others.

Be like the river meandering gently through the meadows. Even though flowing gently, changes occur to the riverbanks.

Gentle flow of water can make great changes, and it starts as a stream and becomes a river, and then the river joins the sea. Likewise, each one of you can make a difference and become your own individual stream and join other streams and tributaries to become rivers of movement. Becoming more powerful by the gathering of each of you. So that you become oceans and change the world, one person at a time.

Yes, you do make a difference, and it starts with you being peaceful inside.

So, develop that peacefulness within; by recognising your God force, your essence, your spirit, your connection with God. Do this simply by remembering your connection with God often. Even a few minutes a day makes a difference. And surely you can give a few minutes a day to remember who you truly are; a spirit in human form. And your spirit will last longer than your human form. So, the truest part of you is your spirit, not your body. But you have to have a body in order to be here, so honour that body as well as your soul and spirit.

Turn inwards each day for a short time to connect with your God because it strengthens you within. It empowers you so much more than the fancy cars and the big bank balance. All these are transient, but you will always be a spirit. You will always continue for Infinity. So, empowering that is so much more important, and is easy to do. Alleluia!

Shalom, Salaam, Auf Weidersehen, Namaste.

Talk 35 With Elaine and Georgie

11th March 2021

(Initially heard nothing for about five minutes…)

Me… I think the lesson here is about being patient. Being patient and trusting. Trusting when the moment is right; not trying to force things to have it your way; but allowing Yahweh (which is another name for God and Spirit) It is rather like that phrase 'Let go and let God.' (Build-up of energy in my chest)

Dear children, do not fret unnecessarily. Do not worry at the small things of life. Conserve your energy to worry about the bigger things in life. There can be a tendency to over-worry, over-fret; to worry unnecessarily; to overthink and overdo. Sometimes just trust in the pause, where nothing happens. Allow yourself to be in the 'space of nothingness'. This is another way of looking at meditation. Just being in the space of nothingness. Allowing yourself to be 'still' mentally as well as physically. Stop the endless chatter in your brain. Allow yourself to be peaceful inside your head. Be calm and trust in the process. Trust in the moment. It takes time for things to occur, and you are in a rush, rushing, doing, achieving. Sometimes allow yourself to be fallow. Slow down and enjoy that, just as much as being busy. Animals take time to lick their wounds and sometimes it is necessary for you to do the same. And sometimes it is just a question of being, doing nothing; just being. And in those quiet times of doing nothing, you can hear us more easily; you 'receive' us more clearly.

Doing nothing also helps develop peacefulness; and when you become familiar with the energy of peacefulness you will find you will want it more and more. And teach your children this same art, for it is an art. Their timetables become so busy, doing this, meeting that, coaching this, training that. Where is the space in their diaries for quiet time, reflective time, 'being' time? This part of them must be developed more. Space and time should be given for this activity of doing nothing. If you're always being busy and in turmoil; then your soul cannot be at peace. So set aside time to be peaceful. All of you at all ages. You will become richer in spirit and in the quality of life by doing this. You will take time to appreciate the small things of life, the blade of grass, the flower. Instead of rushing past it doing something, you will stop and see it; or pause to see it.

Look around you in your homes; are they serene, are they peaceful? If not make them so. Allow peacefulness and harmony to be in your homes because it then encourages peacefulness and harmoniousness amongst you, the ones that live in the home.

Take time to take time. Allow for reflection; allow for creative ideas to bubble to the surface in those moments of peacefulness. Allow communion with your God, in whatever shape that is; whatever religion you choose to believe. Take time to do nothing and value that time. Nurture your soul and yourself with that pause. Like a blanket around you, embracing you; so can the quiet embrace you.

Trust that there are no accidents. That there is a purpose in occurrences in your life. You may not see the full picture in the present moment; but trust that whatever is occurring is meant to be occurring. For God does not allow accidents to happen. There is order in the universe. Even when it seems chaotic; there is still a pattern of order.

Develop the art of serenity; of being serene. Go out into your gardens; not to do something but just to be in them. Stop and smell the roses; cherish the blossoms. Sit and envelop yourself in beauty and harmony and nature whenever you can. Make time for it. Having plants in your house improves the air quality; gives you the visualisation of the green and of nature. And keeps you connected with nature as you nurture your plants within the homes. So instead of going around rushing and doing the cleaning of the house; spend a few moments doing nothing; the dust will be there another time. Make sure you give time for peaceful moments and appreciate them.

Also allow time for communication amongst yourselves; as a family, as a group; as a community. Talk with each other; discuss your feelings; your issues. Let the children feel they are being heard. That you yourselves feel you are being listened to. For this also will give you satisfaction and warmth within yourselves. You do not have children in order to keep them so busy they can't communicate; either with themselves or with you. Take time for family time, togetherness. This enriches everyone and will lead to healthier children, who will become more positive adults. Be responsible as parents; make sure you give time to your children. Don't be so busy doing other things that when they come to play with you; you turn them away. Take time for them; for they will not be with you for long as they will grow up and leave home. So, nurture the time you have with them; treasure that time. For it is a special time for them and for you; and it gives them a strong foundation.

And future worlds depend upon the strong foundation of your children of today. So, you build your future by building your children; their inner strength, their brains, their hearts, their love of self. Not being selfish, but their love of self, their self-worth. You can encourage that as the adult. You can also be an example to your children. By cherishing yourselves, children can learn how to cherish themselves by your example. So, respond to your children; be responsible for your children. Don't just have them;

nurture them. Develop them, body, mind and spirit; so, they become fully rounded beings.

Each one of you can make a difference. So do not do what your neighbor does. See what values you have; what's right for you. And then create that within your house, your home. Question the 'norm'; challenge it. So that we become communities, of love, nurturing, peacefulness. So, stabbing of children does not occur and stabbing of adults does not occur. And there is goodness and wisdom around; not pain and jealousy and hatred and warfare. Warfare amongst children and warfare amongst adults. Become peace-loving; peaceful. Aim for peace in your lives at every level. And this starts with allowing yourself to have a peaceful time each day, to yourself, in amongst your busyness.

Remember there are no accidents, no mistakes. You are not a mistake; you are a child of God doing the best that you can. You may make an error, an odd mistake here and there because you are learning. Forgive yourself for that error, that mistake; and do not judge yourself harshly. Be gentle with yourself and be gentle with your children. Speak softly and tread softly. Make your homes harmonious because your home is your sanctuary, your place of nurture.

Trust the times when nothing happens because even in that sense of nothing happening; things are happening. Unseen but yet occurring. So, trust in the rightness of timings; of occurrences.

And when in doubt, go within for reassurance; spend time communicating with your God.

Amen, Shalom, Salaam, Auf Wiedersehen.

Go in peace and be in peace and give thanks for your lives

Talk 36 – With Georgie

18th March 2021

'Ahlan wa Sahlan.' It is I, Abdullah, bringing you my greeting. And there are no accidents. This you must believe that in the scheme of things there are no accidents. There can be trip-ups, falls and tumbles, but no major accidents. There is purpose in you being here. There is purpose in life. TRUST, a small word but it means so much. Trust that we walk with you. Trust that you will know the right path to take. Trust that everything is perfect in its timing. Alleluia and Amen.

And we give you greetings; The Council of Twelve and Saint Maria Magdalena de Pazzi. And we thank you for being with us and taking time for us.

Perseverance, being determined. Persevering, not losing faith, not losing trust. Trusting that behind the next cloud, the next rainbow will show; all is not lost. There is always opportunity, room for growth, and room for development. Cease to be in fear. Trust the order of the universe. Try to see the bigger picture and do not get lost in the small stuff of life, the miasma of life.

Realise that you are here for eternity; you always exist, in different forms and appearance, but you always are. So, there is plenty of time to correct things that are incorrect and to make good.

This time on Earth seems long, and yet it's small in

perspective of your duration of being. So don't 'sweat the small stuff'. We try to keep up with modern 'isms'. We progress as well. What you, as mankind, knew one hundred years ago is so different from what you know now.

In past times knowledge was lost and had to be re-learnt. And there is wisdom in the Earth; there are signs of past knowledge, wisdom, and innate knowing. Sometimes your science can block out the art form, the folklore and natural wisdom, innate wisdom. You are so busy trying to analyse, synthesise, and look at things microscopically rather than macroscopically. Sometimes you can look too closely at a small particle and only see that one particle and not see the millions of other particles around it, because you are so focused on one small part. Sometimes you do not need to prove; you just need to know and see. See the results, see what happens and trust. You don't have to analyse everything to the 'enth degree'. Some research is good, and some analysis is good. But the scales had been tipped too far in the direction of science, and world wisdom needs to be incorporated as well. Because you cannot see something under a microscope does not mean it does not happen and does not exist. Do not be so limited as to insist that there must be scientific proof. Be willing to understand and know your gut instinct, your knowing what is right and what is wrong, keeping your eyes open to what you see happening. You may not know scientifically what is happening, but if the result is good, why question it? Be open to the wonder of the miracles of Earth, of Nature.

If the natives of a country trust a plant for healing and can show results and traditional medicine, why question it? Use it, use it to your advantage. Gain the wisdom of the native folklore of all countries, the aborigines of all lands. The Amazonians, the

African pygmies, the Australian aborigines, and the American Indians. Recall the herbal wisdom of them all and keep your eyes wide open. Observe what you see and do not negate it because you cannot prove it. Wonders can happen all around you, and yet you can choose to be blind to them, doubt them, or question them. Observe the natural wisdoms and absorb them. Take wisdom from all parts, science, and arts. Embrace both, negate neither; use everything to your advantage.

You all have an innate wisdom which you have forgotten. You have the innate wisdom of your ancestors, and you have the innate wisdom of yourselves, your inner knowing. Take time to remember that inner wisdom. Go into nature and learn, observe. It has major lessons for you to learn and is equally as important as the microscope. Do not eliminate one for the other; embrace it all.

Use everything to your advantage but not to the harm of anybody else.

Be grateful for the wisdom you obtain. Be wise and use it wisely.

Be like a child, with open eyes and wonder, and allow that wonderment to be in your existence each day. The sun rises, the sun sets. Yes, there is a scientific reason for this. However, look at the wonder of the sunrise and sunset. The Earth turns, and yes, there is a scientific reason for that, and yet it is a wonderment. How does it just hang in the skies?

Be like a child. Have an open heart, an open mind. Be happy, be joy-filled and joy full. Enjoy the simplicity of life. Sometimes you need to get out of your heads and into your hearts.

Extend the hand of friendship to everyone.

Some of you can see the Earth folk, the little nature creatures. But you can still appreciate nature, whether you can see it or not, whether you can feel its energy or not. Those of you that can see, teach others how to see the elementals. Appreciate that even rocks have energy and can store memory. You see it with crystals. Use the wisdom of the Earth. Do not sabotage it; take care of it. It is your home while you have a human body, so take care of the Earth. For if you have no Earth, you have no home in the physical matter.

Appreciate each day that you have. Help those in difficulty mentally, physically, and emotionally.

For they are your brethren, they are your brothers and sisters in life.

During this troubled time, take care of yourselves especially. Check on each other and make sure that each other is doing all right.

Be especially careful of the young ones and the lonely at this present time. Reach out to help them. Take time to talk to them, the young and the old. Do not let them become lost and lonely and feeling alone.

Teach them also how to connect with their God selves, their inner beings. Give them that strength of purpose; that inner knowing, so they have a pillar of strength within them as you all do.

Reach out and help your fellow travellers of humanity.

And make sure you take care of yourselves because this is your life, your being. Do not abuse it with drugs and alcohol; do not harm your bodies. Be grateful for them, for they carry your spirit, and without them, you cannot be here on Earth in physical form.

So, nurture your bodies; do not abuse them. Your bodies truly are the temple for your soul, your spirit, your essence, your being, whatever you wish to call it.

You have been given the gift of a body and of life, being present here on Earth. Treasure that gift, nurture yourselves and learn from every possible source. Both arts and science, ancient and new knowledge, and wisdom. Blend it all together and use it all.

Seek wisdom; do not waste your time on frivolity. There is certainly a time to play and a time to be frivolous, a time to just be. But do not waste your brain and your brain power. You are capable of so much, and there is so much available for you to learn from. You are never too old to learn.

Be excited every day that you have here on Earth because it is an opportunity for learning, exploring, and being. Play well, learn well, love well. Be well.

Auf Wiedersehen, Shalom, Salaam, Namaste. Go in peace.

Talk 37 – With Elaine and Georgie

25th March 2021

Dear ones, we are gathered with you. Bringing our greetings and our love, for you are precious to us, all of you. Each one is special in different ways, and we give thanks for your gathering together. It is our pleasure to come, to talk with you and to impart our knowledge and our information, for you have much need of it at this present time. There is so much turmoil going on and chaos in one's mind, churning and wondering in one's mind. Try to keep it simple; try not to overthink but to 'be', in the moment, in this day. Be as centred as you can be in this day, this moment, for this is what you have, right here and right now, in this present time.

You may have regrets from the past that cannot be undone. When you can, make amends to those that you have injured verbally, mentally, emotionally, as you have no idea what will happen tomorrow. The future is open, which is exciting; because if you knew what was going to happen every day, life would be monotonous. So, it's good to be open to what may be coming in the days ahead. And you may certainly put your wishes forward as to what you would like, but it is important to concentrate on today. You have twenty-four hours of this day. Imagine how much you can put into that twenty-four hours. Part of it will be in sleep, yet you can still be creative within your dreams, and we can communicate with you through your dreams. But essentially, you have sixteen hours awake in the day; please do not waste them. Remember to work and to play, to learn. To reach out to others to help them in their day. So, we would implore you when you wake up in the morning; rather than saying, "Oh God, it's morning," to say, "It's morning, thank you, God, for another day ahead. How can I fill it in ways that will help me and help others?" And then be open to ideas that may pop into your brain, those 'aha' moments. Likewise, when you check in with us, for those few moments of meditation and contemplation and reflection, that quiet time where you get to feed your spirit and your soul with nurturing. We can also give you inspiration and ideas during this time. Have fun with your days. Fill them with activities, enjoyment, and nurturing. There is so much you can do in a day, both by doing and by being. When you are sitting, you can be reflective, contemplative, reading, learning, and laughing. And when you are being active, be active. Keep your mind on what you are doing so that you also enjoy that moment equally. Sometimes you are so busy doing that you actually forget what you are doing; you do it automatically. Savour each moment whenever possible. Look around you, observe.

Listen when your children speak to you. Don't just listen to them with half an ear; use both ears and pay attention, for their words have meaning. Children know when you are speaking to them and listening to them; and when you are just paying a little attention. When you take your child for a walk, do not have an earpiece stuck to your ear talking to someone else. Talk to the people you are with; show them nature, teach them, and enjoy their play. Let yourself become part child as you play and walk with them. You will enjoy it, they will enjoy it, and you will have an added richness of the moment, of the time spent.

When you plant a plant in your garden; pay attention to what you are doing; enjoy that moment. Don't have your brain thinking about something else. Be present in the moment, and you will find that each day is more enriched, and you will feel more enriched, more satisfied. You are not here for long, so savour the time that you are here. Make a difference each day. You do impact other people, so have a little forethought before you just blurt out words. Are these words pleasant, loving, harmful, or hurtful? Think a little before you speak. And yet it is fine to be spontaneous when you play. And like a child, keep it simple; there is great wisdom in simplicity. Sometimes the big words can wash over you, and you do not understand. So do not negate the simple message, because it can make deep inroads within you. Listen with the simplicity of children; absorb what you are hearing and what you are reading. Add to your wisdom, to your knowledge. So that when you return to us, you know that you have done well, that you have achieved much, that you filled your life with learning and purpose.

If you are dissatisfied, then search. What is it that you wish? What is it that you are searching for? What are you lacking? It probably will not be a big house or a fancy car. It is more likely to be an emotion, a feeling that your soul is yearning for. If you feel you are accomplishing your soul's path, then continue to do that. But if you feel you are wasting time and not achieving anything, then take a fresh look at what you are doing. How can you change that? How can you be more content with who you are and what you are doing?

If you see suffering, take action to stop that suffering; take a stand. Do not feel that you cannot make a difference. Where you see wrong, try to make a difference. Be responsible for your actions. Be a good citizen of the Earth. You will know if you are doing wrong because you will feel it within. Your heart will not resonate, and neither will your gut feeling, so cease that action, correct that action. You have an inner knowing that can guide you, and you can also choose to ignore that inner knowing, however, by doing that it may well not bring you happiness. Search for that which makes you happy. And as long as it does no one any harm, continue to search until you find what you are looking for and searching for.

Seek for that contentment within your soul, your spirit. That inner peace, that inner happiness, that deep sense of contentment. And be true to yourself. By all means explore, because that is how you learn; that is how you experience. But let your inner knowing and your heart also be your guide. Realise that each one of you is a spirit, each one of you has a soul. Each one of you has an enduring light. So, respect each other; cease the hatred of others because of their colour or their beliefs. Realise you are all searching, all seeking, and that no one way is the right way. Do not be so arrogant as to believe that your belief is the right and only belief to be had. Be flexible and be willing to learn from others of different beliefs, for they also have their wisdom. Again, be good citizens of the Earth. Cease being separate from each other country because you are different countries. You are all human beings living on this planet. Learn from each other's differences; enjoy each other's cultures. Hate no one; love all. Nurture yourselves daily. Give thanks daily that you have life. Be kind to yourselves, love yourselves; be kind to neighbours. No one is the enemy; that is a false belief. You are all trying to experience life on Earth the best you can. You all question why you are here, and that is your responsibility; to try and remember why you chose to come here; What lesson was it that you chose to learn? And again, your inner knowing knows this. So instead of seeking out wise people outside of yourself, turn within.

Check with your own inner guidance, your own connection with your God and your spirit. By all means allow others to guide you and help you, but only you know what you have chosen to do while you are here on Earth. Only you know why you came. And your job is to remember before you come back to us; to remember why you came and what you have chosen to do while you're here. You may not get it perfect, and you may not get it right, but at least if you attempt and try, then you have benefited.

Once you've found IT, whatever it happens to be, do not sit complacently back, and feel like you have achieved everything. There is always more to learn, to develop. And remember to find out how you can help others as well as yourself because you are a community, a community of human beings. You are not separated by colour and by nations. Remember your similarities; you each have a heart, you each have brains, and you each have bodies. Enjoy the body that you have, because it is a gift. Take care of it because it carries your soul, your spirit.

Do not be in a state of fear; aim to be in a state of love, being grounded and being practical. Try to eliminate fear in your life; fear of your boss, fear of not having enough money.

Focus on the good, focus on your love, be heart centred. Yes, you will have times you can't always manage not to be angry or resentful, because you are human. And you learn also with these emotions. But try for the majority of time to be love-filled, to come from a place of heart-filled love, kindness and generosity of spirit. And have fun as you learn. Enjoy each day; savour each day and be grateful for each day.

Amen. Shalom, Salaam, Auf Wiedersehen.

Talk 38 – With Elaine and Georgie

30 March 2021

'Ahlan wa Sahlan.' I give you my greetings, and I wish you well. We greet you and bless you and give thanks for your presence and willingness to meet with us. We likewise ask for healing. You ask how much is us and how much is our subject. We work on this each time we meet with you all. We are becoming closer and clearer and making progress. And we are truly thankful for your help, support, and willingness to be here. This was preordained before you came. There are no accidents and timing is everything, and this timing is perfect. Sometimes things seem out of place and not together. The road can seem to be rough and have obstacles. Sometimes the obstacles are small, and sometimes they are as big as boulders. But you are each filling out your contract with us, your agreement rather than contract; that we came to before you came to Earth. And those of you that sit are as important as the one that speaks; you each have a role. And this work that you do helps develop your spirit, your soul, your wisdom, and knowledge. If you like, you get 'brownie points' for doing this; but this is what you chose to do. Certain planning has occurred on our side. But we managed, and you manage, and we enjoy our time working with you, all three of you.

As we work together, there is a thickening of the bond between us and yourselves and between yourselves. Even with just sitting, you are advancing your soul, your spirit. You are making progress, so never view it as just sitting; you are participating. We use your energy, your essence, your light to help build a connection and build the strength and the power. Improvement and progress, these are things that can be sought for each day. Some days there will be little progress, and other days there will be much.

There is a flow, and as with all flows, they can vary. We liken it to a tributary, a stream. Sometimes the stream runs fast, and sometimes it meanders. And that is perfect; there is no right or wrong way to flow; the flow is the key. Sometimes you need to meander in order to allow rushing to calm; in order to allow the waters to clear and be less muddied. The flow seems to be slightly standing still. Even though that may appear to be on the surface, the undercurrent is still there, still moving, progressing. If it was always a torrent and always in a rush, it would be too tiring. It is like being and doing; there is balance. A slow flow and then a faster flow.

Like children who have spurts of energy as they grow, sometimes they grow slowly, and sometimes they grow quickly. Even as an adult there is still growth going on. Blood cells grow, change, and die, as do the cells of your body. And as the cells of your body die, new ones are created. Even bone grows and is ever being reshaped. And each bone knows what shape it should be, for there is an innate knowledge, a wisdom of the cells of your body. Which cell should point north or south? Or be octagonal? Each cell mixes and blends with its next-door neighbour, just as you should do with your neighbours. Because if there is disharmony, then dis-ease can be created, abnormal growth, negativity.

Seek balance and harmony, both with your neighbours and

with your body. Give your body enough rest time, as well as active time. Allow enough time for sleep, for sleep is healing. Your brain and body need quiet time; when the body can replenish and the mind can freshen, and the brain can freshen. Without sleep your brain becomes harmed. Like everything, it should be in balance. Enough sleep but not too much sleep. Enough activity but not too much activity. You have a left side of the body and a right side of the body. Try and keep those together and in harmony also.

The key truly is balance. Not too little and not too much of anything. Eating and drinking in moderation. Eat enough to nurture, not so much that it causes harm.

Illness can be a reflection of having been out of balance. Too much stress and not enough rest. Or an intake of harmful chemicals and poor nutrition. Try to pay attention to your environment. Try to breathe fresh air whenever possible. Exercise enough but not too much. Too much of anything; even exercise, can cause harm, and can cause added stress to your body. Moderation… If you are working, then make sure you also play.

Pay attention to your heart; your beating heart; your loving heart. A little fastness can be good, but too much fastness and too much stress on the heart is not good for the body. Exercising in moderation helps your heart.

Remember that your heart is not supposed to be kept in an iron cage. It's not supposed to be hidden from others, in defense. Allow its warmth and the love to show. Be soft around your edges whenever possible. Be kind. Be gentle. Be willing to show your humanity. Your vulnerability can even be a strength. When you think of children and babies, they are vulnerable. There is a softness within them that encourages the adult to be soft with them. Nurture them and help them. Remember your inner child, the child that you were, and part of you still is. Be gentle with that child also. Many of you that are all grown up; are often just children that have grown up in body but are still children in their hearts. Be nice to each other, play well with each other, and share the sandpit with others. Do not be so selfish that you grab everything.

Smile at others; say a kind word; be generous. Generosity of time is as important as generosity of money. Your time is precious, so giving time to another is a precious gift. Companionship can be so much more valuable than money.

People lack, through lack of touch, lack of nurture, and lack of companionship. Encourage gatherings of people when you can. Communities coming together, so there is a feeling of connectedness, harmony, and blending with others. Take time to reach out to the lonely. Even young people can be lonely and feel alone. Help reassure others that they are not alone and remind them and yourselves to connect with their God-self, their spirit. To have that inner comfort. Seek to build community, gathering places where the ones that feel alone can feel welcome. Support each other, old and young alike. And remember to support yourself; do not be hard upon yourself, for you too are a child, a child in a grown-up body. Be gentle with the softness inside yourselves.

Give hugs away, and share hugs with others. But do not force yourself upon others; ask permission first, for some will feel too vulnerable to receive your hug. Sometimes just a holding of a hand or a handshake is enough. Touch is powerful; touch can heal. Never cause harm with touch. There is no excuse for that.

Learn to respect each other. Value yourselves and value others. Treat others with respect; treat yourself with respect. You are a living being respect yourself. You are truly a miracle.

Namaste – respect the God in the other person. Recognise the godlike self that you are and the godlike self that the other person is. And honour each other. All life is precious, animals, plants and especially yourselves. Be conscious and aware each day. Be conscious that you have a life that is precious; and that you are precious. And you are enough just as you are, no more and no less. You are enough, and you are blessed.

Shalom, Salaam, Auf Wiedersehen. Go with God's love.

(First time getting together in the same place and not on Zoom. So much more power and feeling.)

Talk 39 – With Elaine

6th April 2021

'Ahlan wa Sahlan.' It is I, Abdullah, and I bring you my greetings, my gift of healing for you. I wish to give you guidance. As the stars twinkle at night, so many that you cannot count them in the skies above and around you, they have a light, a twinkling energy; yet these energies are old, not current. You are seeing the light from many moons ago. Sometimes things take time. Things do not happen in an instant. It takes a while for the light that occurred to actually reach you and be seen.

Value likewise actions that you do now will have an impact many years hence. It may not be in the moment, in the now. Whenever you put effort into something, it's an energy, and energy cannot dissipate; it simply changes. So, they may not see events right now. You have to believe that the events you have today will create a difference and have an effect in time to come. Do not look for an instant reward. Sometimes it needs time to percolate, like a pot of coffee. I spent many years in the desert, in the arid desert. But it was my choice, my learning, and I studied the stars, amongst other things. Stars gave me much comfort because they have been there for so long. Changes occur amongst the stars; vortexes, explosions, collisions, and creations. There is so much beauty in those creations, and there is meaning. So, what you do today has meaning; has a beauty that maybe yet cannot be seen, but trust. Trust that the work you do today will have an effect tomorrow. It may not be literally tomorrow, but it will have an effect in the future.

Allow yourselves to be empowered with the Power of Spirit. I once wandered in the desert, accommodating the heat and the cold, searching, learning and eventually, I found that the learning I was seeking was, in fact, within my soul, my spirit. It took me a long time to realise that the learning was within me and that I had to go within. And to not be impatient; that again to trust.

Trust the Now, the knowing; those inner nudges that Spirit gives you so often. You think that something is a coincidence, yet very often it is not. Indeed, it has been planned by Spirit, by your guides. So, when a coincidence happens and you think to yourselves, "How strange; that was a surprise; that was unexpected." Realise that possibly the event has been planned for and created especially for you; because it was something that you needed to experience. A connection took place that you needed to have. An experience that you have will have taught you something. So, look for the meaning of the experience, the coincidence. It can be subtle; it does not have to be like a loud explosion. Maybe write it down, so you do not forget it. And you can look back and review; at the various occurrences and coincidences that have occurred to you. There will probably be a thread, a common thread through all these coincidences, leading you on your path, your journey. Very rarely is an event occurring by accident. Sometimes even an accident is an event, a preplanned learning experience. For example, we have worked a long time with you, where you have not been aware of us. Yet we have been around you, watching, waiting until you are ready to actively work with us. And we are so pleased that you have come together to work as a team, to help bring our work forward, our message to the planet.

The information we can give is much needed, for there are many lost souls, in pain. Searching for the reason why they are here; What is the purpose of their life? We cannot give them their purpose; they have to learn through experience what their purpose is. We can certainly give tools, guidance, and recommendations as to how to proceed.

We know we ask a lot of you, yet we know that you desire the connection, the knowledge, and the information that we can give you. We would ask you to be persistent, as you have been, to continue on this path with us. As we deepen and connect more closely, we can help more and more.

The main themes will have similarities yet be different. People learn through different explanations. So often the message has to be repeated in different ways so that different people can learn. We keep the message simple because there is much depth and knowledge in the simplicity of the wording, and many more can learn if the words are simple. If we make the words elitist or advanced, then many people will not be able to absorb the truth from them. It will be if you like, 'over their heads'. So, we can help many more souls by keeping the message simple. So do not fret over the repetition that occurs from time to time; there is method in that repetition.

'Ahlan wa Sahlan.' I want to add that you are like jewels, gems; your light glints in the sunshine and you sparkle like the sparkling stars. You yourselves are so beautiful. If only you could see the beauty that you are and the wisdom that you have. Schools need to change and add this knowledge to the children. Teach them how to go within to meditate, to contemplate, and to sit quietly for a period of time to enrich their souls. You will find that the children will enjoy this experience as well as adults. By developing this art of being, you can strengthen your inner being and not be knocked off your base so easily. If you have this inner wisdom and are conscious of it, then you will not be knocked off your base. There will not be so many addictions and unhappiness and pain, both mentally and physically. There will be a lessening of suicides of all ages; there will be less hate and violence because there will be an acknowledgement of the God within each of you because the children will have learnt it at such a young age, then it will be part of them. So, learning to sit and 'Be' is as important as science and languages. Other classes should also teach them about all the different religions and their differences. And more importantly, the common thread that runs through the religions, because there are many common threads. So often, you are too busy looking at the differences to see the commonalities. There is an expression 'walk a mile in my shoes to learn,' so do that. Go to different services of different faiths to experience. And then, when you have experience, you can choose which one you want to follow. And you may find you don't wish to follow any; that you choose to follow your own inner wisdom. You have so much choice, so much freedom. Appreciate what you have and use it wisely.

Differences can work together. Think of the Sun and the Moon; they are so different, and they create different atmospheres, yet together they work as a pair.

Often there is a rejection of people who are different because you fear them. You fear the unknown. So, get to know them and then you will no longer fear them, and you will no longer fight them. Educate your children this way and educate yourselves. It is never too late to learn, to experience.

Keep your eyes and your heart open. Be observant, be feeling; try to find joy and enrich each day. Sometimes there will be profound days, and sometimes there will be simple days, but even on simple days there is a richness of experience. Even if the experience is negative, you can learn from the negative experience. So maybe the negative experience wasn't negative because it taught something. When a child puts his hand on a hot stove, it is a bad experience that they learn not to repeat. So, it was a good experience; unnecessary, unfortunate, but a learning experience.

Adults, please listen to the laughter of children; there is so much joy and high vibration in the laughter of children; it can bring you joy. Never, never cause a child to cry; never hurt them. They are beautiful souls; still all young and they do not deserve your anger, your cruelty, your rage to be deposited on them. And if you do that, then shame on you; for it is a wrong action and there is no excuse. You are bigger than that. You, as the adult, should know better and do better. Just because you are the parent does not entitle you to hit your child or harm it in any way. It is a deep blot on your soul. We cannot emphasise this enough; when you damage a child, it becomes a damaged adult and causes harm because it has had harm done to it. So, remember this, parents, that you are the creator of part of the child, and when you cause emotional damage to that child, you then create a damaged adult that continues to suffer for many, many years beyond the incident that occurred; you caused. Be responsible for your actions. And we say again; you are the adult, you should know better, you *do* know better. Change the pattern. Where you were abused as a child does not give you the right to abuse your child. Stop the pattern and make a difference. Cease the harm.

Dear ones, we do love you. We do care for you and about you. Our words sometimes seem harsh, yet they truly are given in love. We want to encourage you to be happier, more joy-filled and to ensure your journey is more fulfilling. There is so much hurt and searching that we want to try to create a change, a difference for the better, for the betterment of man. Remember! And remember that we do indeed love you and embrace you,

Shalom, Salaam, Auf Wiedersehen, and go with the blessings of your God.

(Elaine had images of? asexual people walking in circles, naked except for loincloths and short conical hats of different colours – green, blue [not purple]. The eyes were closed, and the arms were bent at the elbows with palms facing upwards. The sense was activity but very calm and serene.

The session had several long silences. A minute or two where it felt like the speakers were changing. The feeling was instructional yet loving.)

Talk 40 – With Elaine and Georgie

15th April 2021

Wisdom; being wise. You will fall, but you can rise up again. You can't always be wise because then there would not be growth. Wisdom is a learning process; of gaining wisdom, of gaining experience. If you knew it all, you would not be here. There would be no reason to come here to learn, to gain wisdom, and be at peace with that. Do not be in a rush to always learn. As we have said before, allow for playtime as well as learning time.

Life is an adventure to be enjoyed, to be taken every day. Do not be in a rush to get to the next day; enjoy *this* day. Enjoy the time you have been in every twenty-four-hour day. If you are so busy trying to get to the next day, the next week, the next year, then you miss out on so much richness of today. For example, the Sun shining, clouds in the sky, a light breeze. Savour each moment; savour the richness of each moment. Your path will continue, and you will continue to learn that playtime is also important because you can also learn with laughter and with fun. It does not have to be all serious. The balance that we speak of, time, is a learning and a time for play. Equilibrium, balance, things being equal; partly work and partly play.

Remember to love; that you have children, your friends and loved ones. That you are very close to these different levels of love, all of which have a richness. Rather like the rainbow, the seven colours of the rainbow and they can easily be seven levels of love. Passionate love, spiritual love, serene love, loving your animals, even the love of the freshness of the air. Life should be composed of love. Love, this is one of the most important elements that we have, this essence and energy. Spiritual love and passionate love too. Extremes are equally as important, for without the passion, there would be no continuation of bodies on the planet, bodies containing spirits because there would be no procreation. So passionate love is important, but it is not the beginning and end of all. Love can be simple, enjoyment of a flower, your pet, your child's laughter.

Simplicity of life. Life does not have to be complicated. Sometimes you choose to make it so. Look at the simplicity of the child and be like children. Remember to laugh with the pure joy that children have when they laugh. Sometimes this takes effort because sometimes it can be easier to be serious. When you are feeling downcast, you tend to look down. Remember to look up to the skies. More feelings of joy within you lifts the spirit. Be gentle with yourselves; do not be so harsh on yourselves. You can judge yourselves too severely, and there is no need to do this. Life is an experience, a transition of time when you are embodied in a body. Some of you have a short period of time here on Earth, and others have longer. Enjoy the moment; enjoy the movement of being in a physical body on this planet and plant your feet firmly on the ground. Keep your feet firmly on the ground but remember the sky above. Remember your spiritual connection and enjoy both the solidity of the Earth and the lightness in the spirituality of the universe, being both at the same time.

And when you feel unwell, take time to rest. Too often you push through, thinking it is not important to rest. At times the body needs to stop, and sometimes the spirit needs to pause; so, when you are not feeling well, BE with it. It is in the mind, the heart or the body. Give yourself time to pause, to savour that moment of peace. Like winter, at times it is necessary to go within, to withdraw, to rest. Then spring and summer come along, and it is time to grow, to enjoy the warmth, to enjoy the blossoming.

An equal balance of both is important. Time to express, time to contemplate; it all adds to the tapestry in the richness of life. It deepens the colours of the threads of the picture of your life. Do not come back to us and say, "I wish I had; if only I had done..." Explore life to the full; do not deny yourselves. When you have an urge to explore something, do it, but do no harm to others. Act responsibly and with care; do not crush another. Do not be so afraid that you do not do something you desire. If you desire something, have the wherewithal to do it. If you desire something, your soul is asking you to explore, to have an experience.

We are not talking about material goods; we are talking about experiences. Go and see the sacred spaces on your planet; they can teach you about the history of the Earth; the history of your ancestors. Explore and learn so that when you do come back to us, you can say, "I have had a full life. I have done what I came for. I experienced a lot. I learnt." Because you do not come to this planet to just sit around doing nothing, you come here for a purpose, a reason, chiefly to learn. Do not waste the opportunity of life and what life offers you. Do not sit in a corner, afraid of your own shadow. There is nothing to fear but fear itself. When you do not proceed because of fear, it minimises you. Your spirit has come here for experiences, so experience, explore. And if you fall down, pick yourselves up again.

However, do not force doors open that seem not to open. You will find that the correct way forward is where doors open for you; when movement is easy, opportunity seems to just come. Again, let your inner wisdom guide you. Spending a few minutes each day with us can help keep you on the right path. Be open to our messages, to our guidance. Believe in miracles, believe in coincidences and happenings.

There is a purpose to life; like a mushroom develops, it starts off small and opens up to become like an umbrella so that more of the surface can be shown towards the Sun. Growth, development. Turn your face likewise towards the Sun, towards exploring, investigating. Fungus has a benefit to the planet; some fungus is highly valuable.

Laughter can bring much feeling, much joy. Never be so serious that you cannot laugh. Be willing to laugh at yourself; never laugh at someone else, but laugh with someone, laugh at your mistakes. Laughter heals. Be happy; there is nothing wrong with being silly. Do not take yourselves so seriously. You can easily learn and explore and yet laugh at the same time. You do not have to be like a professor, stuck in a room in a library, in darkness, pouring over words all the time. Yes, learn, yes, explore, yes, take parts of life seriously, but intermingle it with joy and laughter, and play.

Let your life be an experience, not an endurance. You have been given a gift of life; enjoy your present. We need a gift as well as the present, the now, this moment, this day.

Be happy, enjoy your journey, and learn from your experiences. Be kind to yourself, for you are a child of good, of God. As a child of God, it is all right to make mistakes from time to time. So, when you fall, and you will fall from time to time, just rise up again and continue on your journey of life and experiences.

Aim to be content, contentment within and without. Make

your homes places of peace so you can dwell in contentment and harmony. No one is perfect, and no one is supposed to be perfect on this planet, for you are all learning. Do not wait until you get old to experience; to 'retire' before you experience. If you're not happy in an occupation, change your occupation because all parts of life are supposed to be fun and enjoyable. If you feel stuck in an occupation, be like a child and become unstuck. Learn a craft, something different, to develop what your heart enjoys. Do not wait until you retire for you to reach your heart's dream, your goal, for that may be a long time to wait. If you wait too long, you may find that you're not able physically to enjoy your dreams. Try to live your dreams day to day.

Be responsible; a functioning person can and should do good to society. And do not leach society; contribute to society. You came here for a reason. Find your reason; seek for it. Grab every opportunity with both hands. Live your life to the full; be aglow with life. Fill your life full. Marvel at life like a child, with open eyes and an open heart. Marvel over the beauty of a butterfly, a flower. Be open to the joys of living. Spread your wings and fly so that you fully experience life in all its many ways. Be heart-filled and enjoy life and its many challenges and joys. And be at peace. When you are in a state of peace, it is hard to make battle. Check in with your spirit every day so that we may communicate with you and give you guidance. Enrich yourselves with feelings of joy and peace and love and be grateful and thankful that you have been given this gift of life and enjoy it to the full.

Auf Wiedersehen, Shalom, Salaam. Go forth in Peace.

Talk 41 – With Elaine and Georgie

26th April 2021

'Ahlan wa Sahlan.' It is I, Abdullah, here to greet you this day. Greetings, our children, we are the Council of Twelve; likewise, we greet you, imparting wisdom. Never forget we are always close to you. We watch over you and care for you, for you are precious to us. Trust that we are always with you even when you do not sense us. The three of you are light carriers. You carry the light of spirit, and as such, you organise for others, guardians of the light, the light of Spirit.

There is so much beauty in nature and likewise in Spirit. The beauty in our world is indescribable; it is beyond description. Because we have colours that you cannot see in your human form. We have sounds, music which you cannot hear. Tones and vibrations that blend and mingle together. We have ways of learning; through just osmosis, through being permeable, through being open. To us, solving, knowledge, books, experience. You can choose to study as much as you wish or as little as you wish and just Be. The choice is always yours. And sometimes you choose not to learn and just to play and experience. Even with experiences, you love, that is like learning.

There are times when you choose to do more formal learning, using our libraries and our resources. There are Halls of wisdom, innate wisdom that you seek, deepening interests that you have. Like being on Earth, you can choose the way you wish to go, topics that you wish to study. What interests one person does not necessarily interest another, and each learns in their own way. Each has a style of learning, and it is important to remember that children of the Earth. Not everyone learns through reading books, through examinations, through studying textbooks. Some are better with their hands, using their physical gifts, absorbing information through being in nature. All types of crafts are needed. The professor of study and the labourer, each has their own gift to develop, learn and use. Both are needed, so do not praise one above the other. Each has their use; each has their reason for being.

When you come to our world, you will realise the serenity and the peace and love that is present. There is harmony, there is peace-making. You live how you want to live, in homes that you want to have, designs that suit you.

You choose how you wish to fill each day. And you can explore other lands. We really want to let you know how harmonious, peaceful, and loving our world is. We encourage you to try and bring that similar energy to Earth. Be the peacemaker amongst your friends and in your society. Strive for harmony within yourselves, within your homes, and in your surroundings.

There is no need for strife. Strife is often based on ego. They need to be right; then need to overpower someone where there is no need to overpower someone else.

You are all here working out how to be here. While you're here, encourage each other, support each other. Do not fight each other and strive against each other, for it is wasted energy and gains nothing.

Keep it simple, be simple; do not minimise simplicity. If you think about the child who is simple, they are taken care of; people nurture them and help them. So even as an adult you can be simple and open. You don't have to be smart all the time.

Just be yourselves. You are good enough as you are. Be yourself, and you do not have to be perfect. It is all right to make mistakes because these are ways of learning.

Be open to others, not closed. Remember that others also have their struggles, even though they may not be that obvious. Each one of you craves to be loved and accepted. Remember that you are simply children of God in adult bodies. Remember the child part of each person and be gentle with each other.

Give encouragement to others. Extend the hand of friendship and be welcoming to others. Each one of you wants to have a sense of belonging, of being acceptable to all.

All of you play your part; reach out to your neighbours, your friends, children, and the elderly. Be kind, especially to the lonely; of all ages. Reach out and embrace them. Let them know that they are loved and cared for. There is concern for them, that they are not forgotten; be harmonious to them.

And most importantly, be harmonious with yourself because it is hard to be harmonious with others if you are not at peace within yourself.

Aim for a little quiet time each day for reflection and contemplation. Communion with your essence and with your spirit and your God. This enriches you, strengthens you from within, and helps you be in a harmonious, serene state. Remember, you do not have to be pious to be serene. You can be serene and yet have fun. Serenity and harmony are states of being, states of mind, and they give you a positive radiance. A beauty of energy and attractiveness, way beyond good looks and make-up. There is something very attractive about one who is at peace with themselves and living in harmony. Do not be afraid to show that part of yourselves to others. Be an example, be a light, a beacon for others. But do not do it for the sake of others; do it for yourself and your very being, radiance and attractiveness

People will be drawn to you because they will feel good being around you, and it is important for you to feel good about yourself. So be gentle with yourself. You are good enough. You are more than good enough. You are loved by us, and you are a child of God, full of goodness and God essence.

The spark of the Divine is within you. Revere that spark; blend with it daily. Do not abuse your body, which is a temple that houses your spirit. Respect your physical being and thank it for being present so that you as a spirit can be present on this planet. Respect yourself and respect others and see the God essence in them.

Make peace with all and where there has been harm, make amends and become peaceful again. Let go of grudges. The bigger the grudge is, it harms you, not the person that you hold a grudge against. That person may be totally impervious, not knowing of your grudge. Holding a grudge is a negative energy and merely harms you. So, when you have done wrong or harm to someone, apologise. Apologise, whether it is directly to the person or energetically. Life is too short to hold grudges, and how sad it would be if you return to us saying, "If only… if only I'd maintained contact and apologised."

Your friendships, your relationships are important. Value them, nurture them; never assume that they will always be there. Seize each day and live it to the full. Filling out to the full can be full of activity or even just contemplation and reflection or studying another book. There are many ways to fill the day. Value each day and value what you do with each day. Do not waste time.

Fill your days with happiness, with contentment, with enjoyment. You are lucky to be here on Earth. You have been given a gift of life. Enjoy it to the full.

Auf Wiedersehen, Shalom, Salaam.

Talk 42 – With Elaine and Georgie

17th May 2021

Envelop yourselves with love and when we say envelop, be like blankets of love, wrapping around you so that you are totally immersed in love, God energy of love. Imagine this blanket embracing you, enfolding you and remember you are perfect as you are. Let God and us love you as you are. We envelop and surround you in our love. United together in this work. This work is for the good of the universe, and the power of three is powerful. Do not worry about whether you are doing things right or wrong. Just being willing; to be realising that not only are you helping us in our work in the universe, which you are; and also helping yourselves in your growth, your spiritual growth. This was a contract that you made together many moons ago, as we said. You are gaining gold stars by doing this work, and we thank you. And I, Abdullah, want to say that you are much loved, and your travails are much appreciated. There is a long line of people who can communicate with spirit, and you are one of the more recent ones. And the willingness to be batteries is so much appreciated and also fulfils your commitments. In time you will see where your efforts and your works lead to. Trust that what you are doing is more than enough and is much appreciated by us.

The themes are many, but the message is essentially the same. To love one another and to love yourselves. Embrace yourself with love so that you are so full of love that you exude love in your very being without being conscious of it. You simply **are** love, and you radiate that love with all your energetic being. You do not have to go up to each and every person and tell them that you love them. Your loving energy suffices, and your loving energy is continuous and can be continuous.

When things get rough, you reconnect with us. In the moment, it is hard to remember that. Try to remember to reconnect and re-join with us on a conscious level when things seem turbulent. We can give you reassurance; we can help you reinforce the centre of love so that you become strong again and cease the wall of uncertainty and doubt. When you are strong within, you are strong without. Just a few moments a day will help to make you strong within.

Enjoy the simple things of life; let them be sufficient. The bird calls, sunshine, the breeze, the laughter of children, and the patter of rain on a window. These alone can enrich your life and your inner being, giving you more contentment. Yet embrace life to the full, gain wisdom, knowledge, experience life experiences in different places. Enrich your life with the arts, through your creations and sense of God and of goodness. This world is rich indeed, rich with experiences. Embrace it and experience it.

Be consciously aware of what you are doing. Feel the love, be in the moment. Be conscious.

Be loving with your words because words have energy and can harm. So make sure your words are soft and loving, and kind. Remember you are love; be love. Every day check in with us, so you can reinforce this, strengthening yourselves for the day. It also strengthens you for any turbulence that may occur. Sometimes you need to bend with the wind rather than standing brittle against it. If you are too brittle, you can snap in the wind.

So, sometimes, you need to allow yourself to bend with the

wind, and when the wind has passed, you can then stand erect again. By bending, it does not mean that you are not maintaining your desires, your strengths. Sometimes bending is, in fact, a strength rather than a weakness. It is like that phrase 'going with the flow'. Likewise, you would not want to stand getting drenched in the rain. If you can, get cover. Water is good but drowning is not. So, act sensibly in any moment. Do not be too rigid in your stance; that is the **art** of being.

Yet do not be afraid to stand out from the crowd when you have something you want to say, when you feel the crowd is going in the wrong direction. Be brave enough to stand in your light and your power and your strength and resist that kind of negative flow. Because sometimes people are lost in darkness, and they need the 'light' of your being to guide them.

So, when you feel strongly that something is right, then stand up and be counted. You never know what difference you can make, seen or unseen. Know that your actions, your being, your speaking and your doing have an effect.

And when you come from a place of positive-ness and kindness and love, you can do no harm.

You have come with a purpose. Do not deny yourself that purpose. Do not come back to us frustrated by the fact that you have not succeeded in what your aim was. Yes, we will forgive you. No, we will not blame you. You will find that you are blaming yourself. So, be joyful in the moment; be joyful in the fact that you have a life, that you can be creative, that you can make a difference. Yes, you may fail at times. You may perceive it as a failure, but really it is not. Maybe it is simply that route, that passageway that you have to go along; in order to learn something about yourself or others.

This is how wisdom is gained, and wisdom is like a pearl

necklace. Pearl by pearl to make your necklace long, and each pearl may be slightly different. Different colour, shape, and all the shapes are your knowledge, your knowledge base, your ideas, and your actions. You make a beautiful necklace with your creative experiences and your being present here on this Earth. Each necklace will be different because each of you has a different experience and different lessons. Each one is beautiful in its own way. Some will be short, and some will be long. Each of them is perfect; there is no right or wrong. It simply is an expression of your existence, and you are responsible for your actions, your goodness.

If you keep love and goodness as your focus, then you can do no harm. You may go down a wrong passage. Realise that you can always correct that passage and rewrite the way that you go.

Nothing is forever except your existence, your soul. Experiences alter you and this is right because if everything was always perfect in your life, you would get very bored. You would not learn, and so your existence here on the Earth would be rather pointless. Because this is why you are here; to learn and to experience, to grow, not just physically but mentally, emotionally, and spiritually. Becoming who you are, full of experience and wisdom.

Honour your elders. Remember, they have many experiences and memories and can teach you well. Learn to respect and honour them. Listen to the ones that resonate in your soul. If something doesn't feel right to you, then it probably is not right for you; so choose to hear someone else. You always have the right of choice.

Choose to do good, choose to care and choose to love. Choose to include the elders in your society in your actions. Do not keep them in houses that restrict them. Let them become teachers to your children, for you. Just because they have become older does not mean they have nothing to teach and give.

Learn to respect them. Make a difference to just one, if that is all you can manage. Enrich their lives with your company. Bring them into your homes from time to time so that you and your family can appreciate them, and they can appreciate the youth around them. Help them to feel less lonely and alone. Surely you have enough love to go around? Surely you can make some time for them. Remember that doing this will add to the beauty of your necklace.

Show someone that you care and remember to show caring to yourselves. Make time for yourselves. Honour yourselves, for you are all children of God, and you eventually will come back to your spiritual home.

(Georgie 'saw' a man join us to help us. His name was Tom, grey-haired, balding, receding hairline, around middle age. Possibly in his sixties.)

Talk 43 – With Elaine and Georgie

24th May 2021

'Ahlan wa Sahlan.' It is I, Abdullah. I bring you my greetings. We, the Council of Twelve, are here also. We bring you our gratitude and thanks for being here. Mary Magdalena de Pazzi also celebrates being with you, together again. We call you 'spirited ones' because you are spirit. That is chiefly who you are; spirit surrounded by a physical body. Enveloped in a body that can sustain the pressures of the Earth. There is more and more dis-ease, and we want to bring more peace and harmony. There is too much hatred, too much disturbance in the minds of others.

It is so easy to pick up the machines of war, yet you are all spirits, and none of you really want to kill. Truly, it is time to lay down the weapons and for all egos to cease. Realise that you are all so alike. There is no reason to be at war with each other, whether it be for politics, religion, or money. War is merely a habit that you humans have got used to doing.

We do not have war here, while you have too much of it. Learn a better way. Learn to refuse to take up arms. If no one picks up weapons of war, there can be no armies, no forces. Make war unusual rather than usual. So often things result in war, where no one really wins.

People die, people suffer loss, and there is much mourning and bereavement. Wars do not make sense. No one is more powerful than another. They may be for a period of time, and then they lose power. Cease the grappling to gain power. Learn to focus on the love in your hearts, in the loving beings that you truly are and stop harming each other. What a waste of life if you just die. Someone else's policies, decisions that you go to war for. Why? The country does not want you to go to war. You must cease and resist going to war.

Say no; become the peacemakers. Some people might call you cowards, but eventually, they will realise that this is the true way; to be peaceful, loving, and kind. No one gains in war, not really. And whatever they gain is transient, and if it is at the expense of your soul, then why?

If you have to gain power by killing others, this is a stain on your soul, on your spirit. Do you believe that when babies arrive, they are carrying guns? In a state of anger and hate? Of course not, and yet in their vulnerability, they are perfectly protected. People take care of them because they are truly vulnerable. Allow yourselves to be vulnerable, to be soft.

You know it is abnormal to go to war, to be fed loud music and drugs to increase your adrenaline and your hatred. This is not who you truly are. Be the first to stand up and hold out the white flag of peace. If more and more of you do this, then it will be hard for the powers that be to gain armies, enabling them to go to war.

You can make a difference, and you can make a stand. Each one of you can choose to make a difference; can choose to stand and say no. Wars can only end when people stop taking up arms and fighting. This could be a planet of harmony and love and peace if each one stood up in their consciousness and said no. It is not up to others to make a change. It is up to **you**.

Recognise the God self within yourselves, the loving essence that you really are and allow that to reflect to others. Turn the other cheek, open the clenched fist into an open hand. Speak gently and with love. Cease all hatred. Make this world a harmonious, happy place.

Harken to these wise words spoken by one who has great wisdom:

'Peace be with you, my children. We encourage and strengthen your actions and applaud them. Walk with peace in your hearts, be of good cheer and laugh often and love much. Enjoy your journeys, your individual journeys. Do not judge your journey with another's because each of you has a reason to be here, a lesson to learn. So, one journey will not be the same as another. Do not judge one another.

Realise that each of you has different lessons and different pathways. Celebrate the joy of kinship, of friendship, of families and friends. Try to celebrate each and every day. Fill your life with laughter but never at the expense of another. Seek out where you can help another. And be grateful, for you have many benefits in your life; so appreciate them. Your sight, your hearing, your lungs filling up with fresh air, various foods that you eat. It is all an experience. Enrich your experience as often as you can and explore your world. Smile on the lost and lonely; on strangers who walk beside you on the road. Love whenever you can. Hold back on the hasty word, the thoughtless gesture, the careless remark. Be kind with your words; be kind to animals in the kingdom.

Where you see wrong occurring, stop it. Do not walk past, pretending ignorance, for fear of interfering. Be responsible in your actions. When things seem wrong, stand up, and speak out; that is your responsibility.

Be loving as often as you can be. Even when you have to make a negative remark, do it in a positive and loving way.

Choose your words. Words are energy, harmony, and when there is more harmony, the better it is.'

Shalom, Salaam, Namaste. We thank you, we love you. Walk in peace, be at peace.

Talk 44 – With Elaine

31st May 2021

Greetings, children. It is I, Abdullah, come to greet you and to give thanks, as does the Council of Twelve and Mary Magdalena de Pazzi, and we are here to work with you.

(I feel as if I am rising higher energetically. That it has raised up, which is accomplished by a button, to help me to stand up!)

So, by perspective, changes occur depending on the viewpoint. Try not to become narrow in your vision. Be prepared to hear what others have to say, for example, with their different faiths and religions. There are many similar beliefs in different religions. Develop the richness of the knowledge of other religions. See what others face. Just because they are not of your faith does not mean it is not wisdom; there is beauty in their words. Take what you like from each religion and cease to worry about the aspects that you do not like.

It is like an opera or a play; there will be some scenes that you like and some scenes that you don't. They all contribute to knowledge, but you don't have to like all the different scenes. Focus on what you like and learn from it.

Why wouldn't the Ten Commandments or the Pillars of Wisdom each have their truth and knowledge?

Celebrate the differences, learn from the differences, and become wiser with the knowledge. It does not mean you have to follow that knowledge, that faith; just that you learn from it.

Educate your children in all different faiths and beliefs; so they too can learn the similarities as well as the differences. And then they can choose what feels right for them.

Just because you were brought up in one religion doesn't automatically make it the right way to be. It has just been a tradition within your families. So do not continue the habit just because it is a habit. Explore and then choose.

Choose the way in which you want to worship your God. Maybe just by being with your God, and your God may be nature. Choose for yourselves what gives you support in a nurturing, inner strength way.

Do not beat yourself up, do not feel that you are full of sin. Unless you have harmed someone, you cannot be full of sin. Do not allow any faith to tell you that you are full of sin, for you are the essence of God, a child of God. You cannot be full of sin.

Walk in the light of goodness and do no harm to yourself or others.

If you do harm, admit the error of your ways as soon as you can, for you are human and can make mistakes. This does not mean you are full of sin. Likewise, you cannot harm people and then ask for forgiveness when you are about to die because you will be asked to judge your deeds when you arrive with us.

Do no harm to your soul, your spirit, your essence. You came for a purpose, for a reason. Seek that out and try to achieve it.

You are the only one that has perspective about what you came here for, like a butterfly that flits from flower to flower, gathering pollen and nectar. It does no harm to the flower; it simply takes, gathers the nectar, the pollen to enrich itself; feed itself. So, it helps itself and does no harm. It spreads its wings and flies, exploring, flying high, glowing and being beautiful.

Do likewise... spread your wings and fly. Enjoy the

exploration, learning, nurturing, and doing no harm. Reach for the mountain tops and to the depths of the seas. Make your perspective as wide as possible. Being open to the many gifts that the earth has to offer. Expand your knowledge and your knowing experiences.

Enrich yourselves with experiences and wisdom, fulfilment, and contentment.

Be in harmony with yourselves.

Fill yourselves up with learning and fun and play.

Absorb the positive and reduce the negative.

Celebrate the gift of life and living.

The world is full of so many experiences, so much scenery and beauty. Explore as much as you can.

Complete your life choice as much as you are able and live in harmony and peace.

Shalom, Salaam, Namaste.

(Elaine saw one large sunflower – all yellow with no dark seeds, no stem.)

Talk 45 – With Elaine and Georgie

14th June 2021

Breathing is good. It keeps us alive. So welcome friends to come and join us, greetings our children. We are the Council of Twelve and we have Abdullah and Mary Magdalena de Pazzi here also; and we thank you for giving us this time. We give you greetings because greetings are so important. It is like an introduction, a welcoming, an acknowledgement of our presence; us in spirit and you in physical. So, we greet you, and we thank you.

Homilies are important as a way of making things known, as a way of speaking at length. Going into a subject in depth to increase the wisdom of the people who are listening. So, we bring you teachings, homilies, advice, and recommendations. Trust that the information we give you has relevance. It may seem to make no difference as we are speaking. But it will lead to more information and more wisdom. A chance word here or a word there will make a significant difference to someone. You yourselves may not understand the significance of the resonance; that the message can make a difference to some people, you enable us to bring forward this information to help teach your brethren. In the past there was much wisdom and knowledge, but much of it has been forgotten and ignored.

We have said before to study the science and the arts of the ancients; seek their wisdom, their knowledge. Do not assume that because it is in the past it has no relevance now. During the ages, there has been a loss of some of the wisdom that the elders had. Do not assume it is no longer needed because it is ancient history. Remember the period of the 'dark ages' where information was lost. Seek out the wisdom of the Sufis, the Arabs, of the Persians in their time. There was much wisdom and advancement and then it was forgotten; books were lost. Study the rights of passage of the Greeks; study the ancient wisdom of the Chinese. It is like the different faiths and religions; each has a point of wisdom.

Likewise, different nations in the past and their wisdom are lost. Seek it out and add it to your current information so that you can expand your wisdom. Bring ancient knowledge forward for use in this day. Remember that everything is energy and activity. Do not waste the energy of the past. Utilise it along with your current knowledge. Walls were made many centuries ago that today cannot be copied. Learn the science of how they were made; seek out aspects of the ancient ones and some will be useful. Most will be useful, and some will not be. Take what you like and leave the rest.

Expand your horizons, expand your knowledge. Never assume that you know it all, for your bandwidth of knowledge may be very narrow and limited. Like the encyclopedias, there can be so much learnt, so much detail about so many things. Surgeries were done in the past that would amaze you now; the wisdom was forgotten. Seek and learn.

Even children can have a wisdom that you lack, because they look with simple minds, open minds questioning. So do not discount what children say, as there is often wisdom in their words if you have the ears to hear and appreciate. Seek and find; have an open mind. Do not limit your exploration, your research. Absorb everything and then you can choose to limit the amount of information if it has no point for you. But do not limit it for you to receive it. Take everything on board, and then you can sift through the information and see what is necessary and what is appropriate for you.

Keep your eyes open and see the beauty on this Earth. See the petals and flowers, the many colours. So many shades of different colours, like all the greens that are on your planet. All the sunrises and the sunsets; glorious beauty. Open your eyes and see, and take in. Do not just glance and look away. Greet the beauty. Breathe yourself in nature; breathe yourself in the light of the stars; in the moment; really enjoy the rays of the Sun. Glory in the fact that you are here experiencing and learning.

Enjoy the communication with others. You can learn from all ages, children and the aged.

Reduce the number of toxins that you are exposed to. Drink pure water and eat pure food. Cherish your Temple, which is your body. There is too much stress and warfare at this time. Make a difference to your body, your home. Filter information like you filter water. Try to reduce the negative information because the negative information can trouble your mind and increase your stress. So, filter the amount that you receive. Try to have positive harmonics surrounding you, music, conversation, food and your atmosphere.

(A pause, silence and then heard 'Maria Magdalena is coming'.)

My children believe in yourselves. Believe that you have a reason to be. Be gentle with yourselves, be kind to yourselves. Honour your God. Honour your spiritual aspect but equally honour the childlike self that you are. And make time for play; make time for laughter. Enjoy your lives while you enrich them. Life should not be too serious. Balance of work and play, like night and day. Be sure you get enough rest. Your brain, as well as your body, needs time to rest; where healing can take place, regrowth of cells and mending can occur.

So, play and laugh and learn; be kind to yourselves and to those that you meet along the way. When you laugh, listen to the resonance. Listen to the laughter like tinkling bells. Laughter is good for the soul. Be in joy and enjoy yourselves. Do not let your life become a habit, a routine.

Live each day fully. Never wait for tomorrow to come, for it may not. So, enjoy each day that you have, remembering to give thanks for your life and your blessings. Strive to make a difference in your world. Do not wait for someone else to do it. Make the difference yourselves and be responsible for your actions. Make yourselves accountable so that you have no shame in your actions, just happiness and love.

Resonate with peace, the love of God, love of the universe, love of life. You can heal yourselves this way, loving your life. For when you love your life, there is no excuse. So, if you are ill and not well, see how you can make changes in your life and your environment so that you are at ease and in joy, allowing your body to come back into harmony and health.

Respect that you are a living being, blessed to be on this earth. Never assume; never take it for granted. Appreciate the gifts that you have been given. Use them well and wisely. Never try to empower another.

Teach your children well, for they are like little birds fluttering their wings. Treat them gently and with love. Encourage their growth and their learning. They can learn in play, as well as sitting at a desk. Seek out each of their gifts and encourage them to develop their gifts and their interests. Do not try to make them identical. Encourage their self-seeking, soul-searching, enquiring minds. And as we have said before, learn from the aged; they have much wisdom. Honour them. Make time and room for them to be with you. They can teach you much.

Remember that you adults are equally fluttering birds on a journey of discovery. Be kind and gentle with yourselves on your journey. Embrace each day to the full and give thanks for your day, your life, and your gifts.

Blessed be. We thank you and we believe you can get far. We are always nearby.

Shalom, Salaam, Auf Wiedersehen, Namaste.

Talk 46 – With Elaine and Georgie

2nd July 2021

Dear children. We come to work with you today, and we give thanks that you work with us. (There is a gentle energy present in this room today.) 'Ahlan wa Sahlan.' It is I, Abdullah, come here today with Maria Magdalena (de Pazzi) and the Council of Twelve.

(Me talking: It's a real gentle, gentle energy here at this moment; soft and slow. I think it's female. I think it is going to be Maria Magdalena.)

Children, I want you to be gentle with yourselves, kind to yourselves, soft. You can place your foot softly on the ground and have the same impact as if you were stomping on the ground. However, when you are soft on the ground, it is more easily absorbed and accepted by others. When you stomp on the ground, people put up a resistance.

Be happy, rejoice. Rejoice is not a word that is used often. Rejoicing in your lives. The beautiful moments that happen when you least expect. Savour those moments. Let them enrich you. Those unexpected moments that come around the corner. Not things you have planned for, but things that simply become a reality in your life. The unexpected gift was the sea seal (that Georgie had seen in her canoe). There is such a richness, an abundance and joy. And yet so often dismissed, discounted, forgotten so easily.

At night keep a journal where you can write these events down so that later you can recall if you should feel down or negative. Because life is a series of ups and downs; so it is good to recall the ups to help strengthen and reinforce you when you're feeling down, for when you are feeling down, so often it is hard to recall the 'up' moments. It is too easy to sink into the pain and sadness. So, support yourselves with memorizing the ups. Ups and downs are the balancing of life, and that is the essence of life, a balance. The balance of spirit and body that you are, the balance of night and day, ups and downs, harmony and disharmony, expansion, and contraction, the being busy and the just being. Take time to reflect, absorb and appreciate. And remember to be thankful for all the many blessings in your life. And even sometimes the downtimes are blessings because you learn something. You learn another aspect of your character, a strengthening of your soul.

When the river runs it can create a cavern, a gully. Just by the power of the water repeatedly running. Over time a deeper chasm, a deeper gorge can be created, and yet the flow of the river is constant, yet it softly erodes.

So, by walking softly yet persistently, you can make changes. You do not have to stomp on the road to make a change. The very act of softness allows greater change. Consistency is the key.

What change do you want to make in your life, if any? Do not wait until you are dying to say, "If Only…"

If you have a heart's desire, follow It. Live It Now, for Now Is All You Have. Today and Today and Today, not the past, not the future, but today.

Today is where you can make a difference. You can make the changes if *you* think they are required. No one else can do it for you, so you have to do it for yourself.

If there is something hankering in your Soul, attend to it. Make a difference in your life, your Soul, your growth. Be at peace with your decisions.

Do not 'wrong' yourselves. Allow experimentation, exploring, and developing your path.

Do not do change for the sake of change. Change only if you feel you need to.

You are here for a short time. Make a difference. Impact positively upon the Earth whether it is in your gardens, in your houses, or yourselves. Make a difference, a positive difference to your Universe. Do not wait for someone else to do it. No one can do it like you can. You have the power, the drive, and the interest in the change. So, you have an enthusiasm that someone else does not.

And if you are happy then leave it there. There is no need for change if you are happy where you are. But if you are unhappy, ask yourselves why; and then make the change. If you are in a job that you do not like, change it. Do not be stuck in it for fear; fear of what may happen if you leave. Sometimes you have to leave in order to create the space for the new to come in. Do not get stuck in a rut at any age. Life is to be lived fully each day. Life is an adventure. So, rejoice that you have been given the Gift of Life in which to make changes, in which to explore and learn. Make a difference in your life and the lives of others you can help. Look around and see how you can help others with their permission and acceptance. If they choose not to change, it is not your responsibility to make them change. They have to choose for themselves. Only you can change you.

Seek for the beauty in each day. When you wake in the morning, thank God for the gift of another day. If a day seems heavy, give it time and be patient and gentle with yourselves.

Look for the rainbow in the clouds, for it will be there if you are prepared to look for it.

If you are being wounded, assert yourself, for you have the right to be here, and no one has the right to wrong you. You Are a Child of God, and You Are Precious. Believe in yourself. Trust. Live Fully. Embrace yourself and your Soul. Live harmoniously.

Be at peace mentally and be filled with Love.

If you are filled with peace in your heart and your mind, you can do no wrong. There can be no disharmony.

Rejoice in your life and make changes if you need.

Make a difference in your world.

Ahlan wa Sahlan. Go with the Peace of God.

Shalom, Salaam, Auf Wiedersehen. We Love You, and We Bless You.

Talk 47 – With Elaine

21st July 2021

Dear brothers and sisters, our friends, our children. We greet you and welcome you, The Council of Twelve, Maria Magdalena de Pazzi and 'Ahlan wa Sahlan' Abdullah.

WORRY NOT

Do not let the little things of life worry you, for they are here for a brief moment and then are gone, like a blink of an eye. You can spend so much time worrying, but this does not gain anything; it just spends energy unnecessarily. Trust. Rather than worry, trust. Trust that everything will be all right. That there is sense in the madness, that there is a theme to what is occurring in your life. That a moment of confusion is merely like putting the brakes on the car, slowing down just a little before you continue on. Possibly in a new direction, possibly on the same route. Sometimes a little questioning, a little doubt is good; so that you do not go headlong without thinking. But to worry and worry and worry over one issue is unnecessary. You can certainly think about it, consider it, but then trust and let go of the outcome.

Let go and let God. Allow us to help in the perceived way that things are going to go. Sometimes you have to let go for forward movement to happen. Sometimes, by holding on and worrying, you prohibit movement and progress. So, acknowledge, consider, think about; possibly be a little concerned because of its unknown outcome. But trust that if it is the right thing, it will proceed forward. So, release worry and trust. Let go of the worry and allow God to help things move forward. Time, sometimes time is needed; a pause in time or a period of time for progress to occur.

Sometimes you cannot see that perfection has taken place until you look backwards with hindsight. You worry, you concern yourself as the progress is happening, and then once you reach the end of that particular progress, you realise that perfection has occurred. Then you move forward to your next project, your next lesson, your next learning. And even if perfection is not achieved, you still have gained wisdom and knowledge, learning. And maybe you choose a different direction or a different aim or theme, but you never lose experience. And there is always learning and wisdom in experience. How can you learn anything unless by experience; truly learn. Not just book learn but learning in life. Experiencing; having something happening to you. So, all experience, viewed in this light, can be positive because you are adding wisdom to your soul and knowledge. The depth of your understanding is growing. So do not waste time worrying. It is an unnecessary energy. Spend that worry time on something more productive of more use to you and others. Worrying really does not affect the end result; it is not a positive way to spend your energy or your mind.

Learn to go inside and spend some time with us each day. We will help you cease your worrying; we will help to reassure you. We can give you an inner contentment. A ceasing of the restlessness, the searching, the unknowing.

We can give you reassurance, and we might even give you guidance to change direction, to change your focus. Or it may just be necessary for you to go through that path; because again, it is learning.

Do reflect a little time with us in spirit each day. It will strengthen your soul, give you heart, help keep you calm and reassured, centred and contented. It will allow for smoother running of the engine along the way. Like casting oil on the rough waters, it will help to smooth out the turbulence of your mind.

Be at peace within yourself whenever you can be. Life is meant to be peaceful and enjoyed. Life is meant to be a pleasant experience. And you can have as much fun and learn as much by having fun as you can by seriously studying books. Balance of both is good. So, do not be over studious or over playful; bits of each make a perfect blend.

Be 'spirited' in your life. Full of spirit, full of laughter, full of sensitivity towards others. Kindness to yourself and others. Be aware that you are part spirit and part flesh. Each part is important, for one cannot exist without the other. So, enjoy being in a body and take care of that body. Nurture it, fill it with positive foods and water. At the same time, if you were just a body, you would be like an empty shell with no spirit within. So, remember to nurture and love the spirit part of you, the person who you truly are. Not a figure, not five foot ten, but you, your essence, your God-like essence. Respect it, pay attention to it and revere it, but do not become arrogant.

Remember that each and every one of you has a spirit, is a spirit and is a child of God. Respect yourself and respect others, for you are all beautiful beings existing on this planet Earth. Cease warring with each other. Love and respect each other. Hold yourself in the essence of peacefulness, for when you are peaceful within, it is hard to go to battle without. Battling with one of your fellow brothers or sisters is not good, not positive, and should be discouraged.

Harmonious togetherness, dancing together, living in harmony together, cherishing each other. That is what is important in this life. Be of good cheer, be happy; enjoy your life fully. Learn well, study well, play fully and laugh often. Let your whole being be full of laughter and joy. Smile at your brethren, even if you do not know them. Smiling at another is a gift; for them and makes you feel good also.

Embrace yourself and embrace others. Do not be selfish yet take care of yourself. For when you take care of yourself, it is then easier to help others with a free heart, open hand and calm mind.

Be harmonious with yourself, and you can achieve that more easily by communing with us daily for a brief period of time. Connecting with us, acknowledging the spirit part of you. Also then go forward and enjoy being a human being in a body, doing things you cannot do in spirit. Experiencing life on planet Earth. Live responsibly, play responsibly. Do no harm to others and do no harm to yourself. For you are a dear child of God and the universe, much loved by us.

When you wound yourself mentally or physically, you wound us, for you are given the gift of life to enjoy it fully. To experience the ups and the downs, to mature, to grow, to become wiser than you currently are.

Never cease to grow, to learn. Life is a growth experience. You can learn until the day you die, even if you die after becoming one hundred. Life is always a learning experience.

Seek for the positive in your life. By focusing on the positive, you can then appreciate more what is around you. What is occurring and how fortunate you are. Because there will always be others that are less fortunate than you, so try to stop feeling sorrow for yourself if you do. Look with different eyes, within and without. Appreciate the many things you have in your life that maybe you take for granted. Look around with broader far-seeing eyes. You are fortunate to have been given time on Earth. Enjoy it to the maximum.

Never let yourself get bored. There is so much you can do in this life. A state of boredom merely means that you have closed your mind to other opportunities, gifts, and choices. Are you so much in fear that you have ceased to live fully? Life is not just a period of time to exist in. Life is a period of time to explore in and live in fully.

Take a deep breath in and inspire yourself. Expand your universe, expand your experiences.

Life is for living fully, not for dying quietly. Not for just existing until you die.

How much better to live fully, experience, than to merely exist. You have the choice.

You have the choice… choose wisely.

'Ahlan wa Sahlan.' Go with God. Go with goodness in your heart.

Shalom, Salaam, Auf Wiedersehen, Namaste.

Talk 48 – With Elaine and Georgie

28th July 2021

'Ahlan wa Sahlan.' It is I, Abdullah, come to speak to you this day. Welcome, dear children, as we sit together, united in harmony. Blessed Be.

Sometimes it is hard for you to see the fruits of your labours. You speak and wonder what will happen to those words. Trust in the moment, and this is true for life. Trust in the moment; trust that you are being led. Trust in the power of your connection with spirit. You are all well-loved and we watch over you. Be at peace in your soul. Do not let yourself be troubled. Recognise that you are truly blessed to be here on this planet. Resonate with us each day. Recall that you are both spirit and body and nurture each. Have an open mind and explore and learn. Enrich yourselves with experiences and knowledge. You are a part of the universe, an infinite part yet a necessary important part. Do not doubt the rightness of you being here, both here in this room and here in this world. There are no accidents. Things occur that are meant to occur. Sometimes they may not be to your liking, but sometimes they are necessary, and we have told you before, it is all a learning experience, strengthening your soul, deepening your experience. Give yourselves the few moments of quiet where you can meet and blend with us.

Celebrate being alive, the fresh air, the sunshine, the rain, the laughs and sometimes the tears. It is all experience, all learning.

You seek wisdom; that is why you came here for experience and learning. Sometimes it is when the road is most troubled that you learn the most. When you get lost, look into the skies, and see the stars and realise that we are all around you. Sometimes not seen and sometimes seen; you are never left alone. We observe. At times we try to hold your hand and support you more closely. But it is important for you to have free reign. Experience the freedom of being on this planet and having choice. You are never tied down by us; we simply try to help you along the way from time to time.

The universe is like a myriad of stars and planets interweaving. Trust that when you are ready, you will come back to us, casting your body off like an overcoat. Like unzipping a suitcase or an overcoat, allowing your true essence to slip out of it and come home to us, to your family that have passed before. To your loved ones that have passed, for nothing is wasted. When you see your loved ones go before you, realise that you really will meet again, so you never lose your loved ones.

Yes, you may not see them physically, but they are still around, keeping a concerned eye over you, wanting you to be happy, wanting you to not over-grieve, over mourn your losses. You will feel the loss. You will feel the tears and sadness, but do not bury yourself in that sadness. You have your own life's journey, and it is important that you do not waste it; but that you live it fully.

So, move on with your life, with your fond loving memories, remembering that you will indeed reunite when it is your time to come home. Then you can celebrate your reunion with your loved ones; you can share your experiences; you can rest and play. Then when you choose to, you can start to relearn; either here at home or else making another journey elsewhere. It is always your choice, yet we will offer guidance like we offer guidance when you sit with us in your physical life.

Is it so much to ask that you spend fifteen to twenty minutes each day with us in that twenty-four hours? Do not try to do it when you are falling asleep, because you will fall asleep, and you may remember what was said or learnt as you dream. Allow yourself those few minutes when you feel fresh and rested when you can be quiet. Do allow yourself to go within, to commune with us. Sometimes the communion will feel clear and sharp; sometimes what you hear or ask for, you may not be experiencing in reality for a few weeks or months.

Yet we do hear, and we do receive your thoughts, your requests.

Sometimes your requests are answered and sometimes they are not; you have to trust. Sometimes when your requests are not answered, it is because it may not be the right thing for you, for your highest good. But we do listen, observe, and take counsel.

We observe your progress, and we applaud you for your progress, for you are all doing so well. We know you have doubts, questions, and queries. Pause for a little while in that time of communing with us, and not speak or think; just *allow the silence*.

Let yourselves *be* there so that you might hear the messages, the words. You might allow your brain to receive the ideas, the influences that we pass to you. Because sometimes, when your brain is so busy, we cannot be heard. We never shout; we never say negative things. So should you hear that; it is not us, not spirit, not the ones that you love.

We guide with a gentle hand, a soft voice, and to hear the soft voice you need to be quiet in your mind. This is not always an easy task, but practice will help. Allow yourselves to be enriched by us, with our messages, our reassurances and love.

When things seem very dark, realise we are with you. Be gentle with yourselves, take a deep breath and try to spend some quiet time with us. Look up to the heavens, to the skies and the stars.

Realise the magnificence of the universe, and that you do count, you are important. Do not waste your life until you have lived it fully, for that would be a tragedy for your families and your loved ones, but also for yourself. Although in the moment, it might seem black and dark, there is always a light at the end of the dark tunnel. Things do change; remember that people love you. Do not deprive them of your company, your presence, and your love. Keep walking forward, experiencing. And the pain and the darkness will disperse if you allow it some time.

Likewise, when you die, you will see a light at the end of the tunnel as you come home. It is a different kind of tunnel and a different kind of light, yet the similarities are there.

When you are leaving Earth, when you are ready, and only when you are ready, and have fulfilled yourself to a maximum; then you come home to us. We guide you home, embracing you with open arms and joy and celebration.

Celebrate being alive, for this is a gift. Do not cast the gift away; embrace it openly. Allow your soul to expand and learn. Do not limit yourselves. Seize everything for your opportunity, as long as you do no harm.

Be happy, be content; breathe deeply and love much. You are truly a child of the universe, and a child of God, of good. Enjoy your walk on Mother Earth. Do not be in a rush to come back to us, for you have a life to lead and to live it fully. Do not waste the opportunity and gift that you have been given.

There is plenty of time to celebrate when the time is right for you to return to your true home with us.

Auf Wiedersehen, Shalom, Salaam. Go with love in your hearts.

(Georgie 'saw' a Marlin fish with beautiful shiny silvery scales, swimming and leaping happily in blue-green waters.)

Talk 49 – With Elaine

5th August 2021

(Long pause/silence initially.)

Our Father is much pleased with you and your progress and your commitment to us. Alleluia in the most highest. 'Ahlan wa Sahlan.' It is I, Abdullah, here with you this day. And we bring you our greetings. The Council of Twelve and Saint Maria Magdalena de Pazzi are also here. We honour you muchly for you are doing good work. We want to bring you faith and encouragement that you are indeed doing well, and we give you thanks.

It is in the irony of the world and the irony of events that you must look to with an open eye. Sometimes it is in hindsight that you see the wisdom you have obtained. Try to view your life and your events with open eyes and an open heart. Realising in the moment the beauty of life. Not waiting for the hindsight but recognising in the moment and appreciating everything around you. The laughter of children, the joy of looking at a rainbow. The sun shining on you, keeping you warm, and the darkness, allowing you time to sleep, to rebalance yourselves.

Encourage yourselves to grow and learn. Never let a day go by without learning something. Even how to put a piece of thread through the eye of a needle is an achievement. So do not disregard the little things you do each day, and, maybe in the evening, before you go to sleep, allow yourself to recall the events of the day, the large and the small, as a treasure chest that you are filling up with learning, laughter, and joy. Give yourself a hug when you go to sleep at night. For you deserve a hug and if you have no one else to hold you, then hug yourself.

Learn to love yourself, not in an egotistical way, but in a loving, gentle, and fulfilled way. Be gentle upon yourself and walk gently through the Earth. You do not have to barge your way through life. Enjoy the journey of your life. It is not all about getting from A to B and focusing on B so much that you ignore the journey from A to B. This can be a journey done in a day or the journey of your life. Enjoy the trip, the way through the journey. Celebrate smiling at someone on your path. That smile may be the biggest gift you can give someone. It may change a person's perspective of their life. Look into the eyes of your fellow traveller on their journey and acknowledge their divine being within, as well as acknowledging the divine being that you are. That is why you deserve to give yourself a hug every day.

You are not an accident; you are meant to be here and to learn and to love.

Try to be of service to others. Look for a way where you can help others, whether it is teaching, nursing, or healing; even playing with children can be a large help. Children learn through play.

Try not to neglect your children. Try to not push them away because you are too busy. Give them time, not just presence. Time is so valuable for children. A day to them is like the universe. Spend time, quality time with your children. Not just sitting in front of a television or letting them play while you focus on your phones. Focus on your children. When you go for a walk with them, talk with them, play with them. Teach them the leaves of the trees and the flowers on the ground. Rather than focusing on your phones and your other friends, be present with your children. That is the biggest present you can give them, your presence, your focus on them. Not to make them arrogant and selfish, but to let them know they are being nurtured and loved and are of value. Encourage their souls to develop. Nurture them, treasure them, for they are a gift that has been given to you. They have chosen to come to you, so treasure them. Enjoy them while you have them. Some of you will have them all the days of your lives, but others may drift away.

Do not hold them back; do not crush their wings. Allow them to learn to fly, like the dragonfly, like the bird. Do not hold onto them when they grow.

Do not say to yourself, "I wish I had more time." Maybe you did have time; but chose to use it in other ways, other distractions. You are their foundation block. Help them to have a secure foundation.

Never shout at children, for they are delicate beings and wound easily with words. And children, like you, will make mistakes. That is part of growing, of learning. Enjoy your children and be with them fully. Children need to be heard, to have their questions answered. Encouraging their enquiring minds to grow and develop. And likewise, you as adults should continue to learn and develop. You are never too old to learn.

Allow the warmth of the sun to settle around your shoulders. Breathe in the fresh air. Look into the face of a flower and reflect. Reflect on the beauty of the flower and yourself, and never say that you are not beautiful; because you are a beautiful soul, a beautiful being. See the goodness and the god in others and yourself.

Try to have a laugh each day, at the very least. A laugh is like an internal massage, increasing your vibrations, lifting your spirit and your energy. Be harmonious with others and try to be harmonious within yourself. Have learning time, playing time, and reflecting time.

At the top of the hill, look at the outside edge of a hill and how it meets the sky. How the ground, Earth energy, meets the sky and the Universal energy; they intertwine. You are part of both, Earth energy and Universal energy.

So let yourself be centred in the Earth, grounded, walking firmly and softly. Yet, at the same time, being aware of the universe, the spaciousness of the world, the intertwining of everyone's energy and your connection with the universe. The soul that you are and the physical body that you are like the Earth and the Sky, they blend together. There is a seamless intertwining of the two.

So be neither too grounded, heavy, and serious, nor too airy fairy and not in reality because you have come to Earth to mix the two. To be in reality and at the same time be aware of your godlike self, the godlike part of you. Balance again. And so the spiritual soul part of you and the physical part of you are a balance. Like night and day, like work and play; being harmonious.

If you are wronged, you have the right to make yourself known, to make your hurt be known; so that it does not occur again. And also, if you should cause a hurt, repair it as soon as possible. You all are human, and words can come out when you least expect that hurt someone else. Rectify it as soon as you can. Make peace with the other person as soon as you can. None of you is perfect, and if you were perfect, then you would not be present on Earth, for the Earth is a learning experience. So, recognise that you are like a child at whatever age, learning and developing. Making mistakes, making progress. Do not be hard upon yourselves and never be hard on another.

Lay your weapons of war down. End wars by not picking up arms. If no one goes to war, then there cannot be a war. If you are asked to go to war, ask, "Why?" Question it always. It is never for the honour of your country. It is usually about misguided power and desires. It comes from ignorance, not knowledge. It comes from fear-base rather than love-base. So do not pick up arms of war; do not engage in war or battle.

Let this planet become a place of peace and harmony. And you have the ability and the responsibility to do that, each and every one of you. Mothers, do not let your sons and daughters go to war. Teach them that it is not right. There is never a good reason to go to war. Always choose discussion, negotiation, and compromise, for otherwise you will destroy yourselves and what is the point of that? You are here to learn, to love, to be happy. Why let war shorten your life? No one is ever a victor. Walk with peace in your hearts and open hands, with smiles in your hearts and on your faces. Enjoy being here. Walk lightly on the surface of Mother Earth. And do no harm to nature, or to people or to yourself.

Love yourself and be thankful that you have a life to enjoy here in the physical. You are never alone, and you are much loved. By us in spirit as well as families and friends. And you are all the family of man, woman, child. Enjoy your community, your neighbours, your village, your town, wherever you choose to live.

Reach out to your neighbours and to strangers. Keep good communion with your friends, for friends are valuable. And you may have many different kinds of friends as well as your families, and they are a good support for you. Make sure that you are a good support for them, and if you do not feel supported,

then let go of that friend, for the time together may be passed.
Do good to each other and do good to yourself.
Here endeth the lesson for today.
'Ahlan wa Sahlan.' Walk in peace. Be in love; of yourself and others.

Shalom, Salaam, Auf Wiedersehen.

(Elaine 'saw' a brown wooden cross with a grey metal middle part. She also felt a heaviness in her left hand.)

Talk 50 – With Elaine and Georgie

24th August 2021

'Ahlan wa Sahlan.' It is I, Abdullah, and we, the Council of Twelve, and Maria Magdalena de Pazzi is also with us. We give you many greetings. Greetings of joy, of love, of harmony and many thanks. Fifty is a lot, and yet there is so much more we can still teach you. Thank you for all that you have done for us.

Wonderment! Be in a state of wonder. Wonder what is in your future; wonder at the fact that you live on Earth, open to the daily miracles that are around you.

You are here because of a meaning. Your presence here is not an accident. Your presence here is meant. Timing is everything.

Our many lessons may seem a lot, yet we have covered just a mere part of what we can impart.

Please be in a state of wonderment. Be open to miracles occurring, and these can be quiet miracles. It does not mean that the Sun has to be eclipsed by the Moon so that brightness becomes darkness briefly.

Miracles can be subtle; the first gasp of a baby being born; the landing of a butterfly on your hand. When nature reaches out to you and touches you, it can touch you physically, and it can touch you emotionally. So have the eyes of wonderment for nature as well.

Be observant whenever you can and be appreciative of the

many gifts that are around you.

So often you walk with eyes shut. Practice keeping your eyes open. Observe, be aware and be filled with wonder. Each day can be a joy if you choose to focus on that viewpoint.

You can choose to worry about all the stresses that this life brings and all the troubles of the world. But this just brings you down and makes you feel sad, overwhelmed, and unable to do anything about it.

Wonder at the bird's call. Wonder at the butterfly developing from its chrysalis.

So many miracles go by unseen, unnoticed. Make yourself focus on the joy and the positivity.

This does not mean that you are ignoring the problems. It simply means that you are choosing to **focus on the more positive vibrations.** By doing so, you will not be overcome, and you can make changes in your universe. Your universe may be as small as your house, your garden, your circle of friends. Make an impact in those areas that you have a purpose with, a function with, where you can make a change.

The more positive areas of the Earth that are present will help **keep back the negativity and the fear** of other places.

Make changes when you can. Create Heaven in your area. Reach out and help those that you can. Make a difference in your world, your piece of it. And try to be at peace within that framework.

Beloved, be at peace within yourselves. Walk in harmony whenever you can and speak in harmony whenever you can. Place that peaceful harmonic in your surroundings. And these waves of harmony and peacefulness can have an impact on others, and may even pass along to the troubled areas and help to smooth and minimise the troubles.

Where you see hatred, try to bring love into that arena. Thoughts can have a positive impact; prayers for others can help. Never underestimate the power of prayer. These are powerful vibrations and have an impact on the energy of the Earth.

Harmonise your soul with us from time to time, especially if you feel weak, weakened, down, or depressed. We know it takes an extra effort to raise your soul up when you are feeling depressed. But the effort is worth it and can help to raise you up more swiftly and with less distress.

Harmonise with beauty, with art, with music. Focus on these miracles; sounds that are created from nothing, pictures created from nothing that can fill the soul with delight and happiness.

Allow the part of yourself that can be creative to shine forth. Do not discount your abilities, for you all have abilities that show in various ways. Nourish those abilities, for they are God-given, and you chose them to have here on earth. See your strengths and not your weaknesses. Focus on the inner strength that you have.

Be present in the dawn of the day and remember what opportunities you have in the next twenty-four hours. Each day is a fresh start, full of opportunities for you to explore. Seize the day, seize the hour, the minute. Do not waste your time staring at screens that mean nothing. Look to where you can be creative. Spend a little time communing with us, and relaxation is good, in proportion. Remember to commune with others, with other human beings that are in your space, near you. Your children, your friends.

Do not zone out into the screens. Use them for learning, use them for relaxation, but maintain a balance of productivity as well as rest, of learning as well as play.

Spend time in good company, in positive company. Try to minimise the negative person, the negative news. You always have a choice as to how you spend your time. Choose wisely; be smart in your choices; be selective. Learning and playing are equally important.

Enjoy being in a physical body and enjoy the spiritual aspect of yourself. Nourish both for both are important. Love yourselves and love others. Be gentle and kind to yourselves and others. Nurture yourselves in healthy ways. Do not overdrink, overeat, or numb out with drugs and unhealthy substances.

Be alive while you are alive. Cherish your lives, your bodies, your spirit, your essence, for you are valuable and have value. Never doubt that. There is meaning to why you are here: go and discover that meaning. Never give up before the time is right for you to leave your body. Live life to the full. And again, be in joy and wonder. Because you have been given a great gift, the gift of life, live it to the full.

Ahlan wa Sahlan. We greet you, and we leave you for this time.

Shalom, Salaam, Auf Weidersehen, Namaste. Go forth in peace and love and harmony.

THE END... FOR THE MOMENT!

Notes

Other Books by Carolyn Hornblow

After a Life Threatening Diagnosis... What's Next?
ISBN 9780367773564
Routledge: Taylor and Francis Division

The Heart in the Abbey' (about Dervogilla and John Balliol)
by Jane Gregor (pseudonym)
ISBN 978-1897604311